A s YOU FEEL THE
TIMBER OF THE CROSS
AND TRACE
THE BRAID OF
THE CROWN AND
FINGER THE POINT OF
THE SPIKE—

PAUSE AND REMEMBER.

H E DID THIS JUST FOR YOU.

Max Lucado

TO:_____

FROM: _____

HE DID THIS JUST FOR YOU
Copyright © 2001 Max Lucado
Published by Blessings Unlimited
Pentagon Towers, P.O. Box 398004
Edina, MN 55439

Taken from the book *He Chose the Nails*
by Max Lucado, published by Word
Publishing, www.wordpublishing.com

Design by Garborg Design Works

Scripture references are from the following sources:
The Holy Bible, New International Version (NIV). Copyright © 1973, 1978, 1984 by International
Bible Society. Used by permission of Zondervan Publishing House. The Living Bible (TLB), copyright
© 1971 by Tyndale House Publishers, Wheaton, Ill. Used by permission. The Message (MSG), copy-
right © 1993. Used by permission of NavPress Publishing Group. The New King James Version
(NKJV), copyright © 1979, 1980, 1982, Thomas Nelson, Inc., Publisher. The Message (MSG), copy-
right © 1993, 1994, 1995, 1996. Used by permission of NavPress Publishing Group. The Holy Bible,
New Century Version (NCV), copyright © 1987, 1988, 1991 by Word Publishing, Dallas, Texas 75039.
Used by permission. The Holy Bible, New Living Translation (NLT), copyright © 1996. Used by permission of Tyndale House Publishers, Inc., Wheaton, Ill 60189. All rights reserved.

ISBN 1-58375-890-9

January 1

Long ago, even before he made the world,
God loved us and chose us in Christ to be holy
and without fault in his eyes.
His unchanging plan has always been to adopt us into
his own family by bringing us to himself through Jesus Christ.
And this gave him pleasure.

EPHESIANS 1:4–5 NLT

Can you imagine your final message to those you love? Your last words with a child or spouse? How would you say your final words? Deliberately. Carefully. Most of us have only one chance to make our last statement. As deliberately as you would choose your last words so your Father left this message: "I did it for you. I did it all for you."

December 31

For Christ also hath once suffered for sins, the just for the unjust, that he might bring us to God, being put to death in the flesh, but quickened by the Spirit.

1 Peter 3:18 KJV

January 2

So we praise God for the wonderful kindness he has poured

out on us because we belong to his dearly loved Son.

He is so rich in kindness that he purchased our freedom

through the blood of his Son, and our sins are forgiven.

EPHESIANS 1:6–7 NLT

December 30

Who is a God like you, who pardons sin and forgives the transgression of the remnant of his inheritance? You do not stay angry forever but delight to show mercy. You will again have compassion on us; you will tread our sins underfoot and hurl all our iniquities into the depths of the sea.

Micah 7:18-19 NIV

January 3

God's secret plan has now been revealed to us;

it is a plan centered on Christ,

designed long ago according to his good pleasure.

And this is his plan: At the right time he will bring everything

together under the authority of Christ—

everything in heaven and on earth.

EPHESIANS 1:9–10 NLT

Knowing his last deeds would be forever pondered, don't you think he chose them carefully? Deliberately? Of course he did. There were no accidents that day. Jesus' last moments were not left up to chance. God chose the path; he selected the nails. Our Lord planted the trio of crosses and painted the sign. God was never more sovereign than in the details of the death of his Son.

December 29

God was pleased to reconcile to himself all things, whether on earth or in heaven, by making peace through the blood of his cross.

Colossians 1:20 nrsv

January 4

Because of Christ,

we have received an inheritance from God,

for he chose us from the beginning,

and all things happen just as he decided long ago.

EPHESIANS 1:11 NLT

December 28

We do not have a high priest who is unable to sympathize with our weaknesses, but we have one who has been tempted in every way, just as we are—yet was without sin. Let us then approach the throne of grace with confidence, so that we may receive mercy and find grace to help us in our time of need.

HEBREWS 4:15-16 NIV

January 5

When you were spiritually dead because of your sins and because you were not free from the power of your sinful self, God made you alive with Christ, and he forgave all our sins. He canceled the debt, which listed all the rules we failed to follow. He took away that record with its rules and nailed it to the cross. God stripped the spiritual rulers and powers of their authority. With the cross, he won the victory and showed the world that they were powerless.

COLOSSIANS 2:13–15 NCV

December 27

Troubled about your final moments? Leave them at the foot of the cross. Leave them there with your bad moments, mad moments, and anxious moments. About this time someone is thinking, "If I leave all those moments at the cross, I won't have any moments left but good ones." Well, what do you know? I guess you won't.

So if anyone is in Christ,
there is a new creation:
everything old has passed away;
see, everything has become new!
2 Corinthians 5:17 NRSV

January 6

WE ARE AT OUR BEST
WHEN WE ARE GIVING.
IN FACT, WE ARE MOST
LIKE GOD WHEN WE
ARE GIVING.

See if I will not throw open the
floodgates of heaven and pour out
so much blessing that you will not
have room enough for it.

MALACHI 3:10 NIV

December 26

We throw open our doors to God and discover at the same

moment that he has already thrown open his door to us.

We find ourselves standing where we always hoped

we might stand—out in the wide open spaces of God's

grace and glory, standing tall and shouting our praise.

<small>ROMANS 5:2 MSG</small>

Oh, the things we do to give gifts to those we love. Every Christmas, every birthday, every so often we find ourselves in foreign territory. Grownups are in toy stores. Dads are in teen stores. Wives are in the hunting department, and husbands are in the purse department. And we'd do it all again. Having pressed the grapes of service, we drink life's sweetest wine—the wine of giving.

January 7

If you remain in me and my
words remain in you,
ask whatever you wish,
and it will be given you.

John 15:7 NIV

December 25

Nothing can ever separate us from [God's] love. Death can't,

and life can't. The angels won't, and all the powers of hell itself

cannot keep God's love away. Our fears for today, our worries about

tomorrow, or where we are—high above the sky, or in the deepest

ocean—nothing will ever be able to separate us from the love of

God demonstrated by our Lord Jesus Christ when he died for us.

ROMANS 8:38–39 TLB

January 8

Have you ever wondered why God gives so much? We could exist on far less. He could have left the world flat and gray; we wouldn't have known the difference. But he didn't.

The whole earth is full of his glory.

Isaiah 6:3 niv

GOD PROMISES TO COME
AT AN UNEXPECTED HOUR
AND TAKE US FROM THE
GRAY WORLD WE KNOW TO
A GOLDEN WORLD WE
DON'T. BUT SINCE WE
DON'T, WE AREN'T SURE WE
WANT TO GO. WE EVEN
GET UPSET AT THE
THOUGHT OF HIS COMING.

December 24

*Jesus said, "Don't let your
hearts be troubled.... I will
come back and take you
to be with me so that you
may be where I am."*

JOHN 14:1,3 NCV

January 9

He splashed orange in
the sunrise
and cast the sky in blue.
And if you love to see
geese as they gather,
chances are you'll see
that too.

_The heavens tell of the glory
of God. The skies display his
marvelous craftmanship._

Psalm 19:1 NLT

December 23

Blood he bled for you. The spear he took for you. The nails he felt for you. The sign he left for you. Knowing all he did for you there, don't you think he'll look out for you here?

God did not keep back his own Son, but he gave him for us. If God did this, won't he freely give us everything else?

ROMANS 8:32 CEV

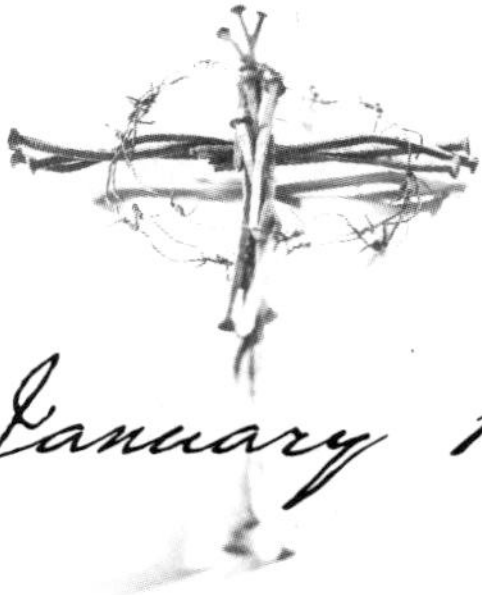

DID HE HAVE TO MAKE THE
SQUIRREL'S TAIL FURRY?
WAS HE OBLIGED TO MAKE
THE BIRDS SING?
AND THE FUNNY WAY
THAT CHICKENS SCURRY
OR THE MAJESTY OF
THUNDER WHEN IT RINGS?

*God's voice thunders in
marvelous ways; he does
great things beyond our
understanding.*

JOB 37:5 NIV

NEXT TIME YOU'RE
WORRIED ABOUT YOUR
HEALTH OR HOUSE OR
FINANCES OR FLIGHTS, TAKE
A MENTAL TRIP UP THE HILL.
SPEND A FEW MOMENTS
LOOKING AGAIN AT THE
PIECES OF PASSION. RUN
YOUR THUMB OVER THE TIP
OF THE SPEAR. BALANCE A
SPIKE IN THE PALM OF YOUR
HAND. READ THE WOODEN
SIGN WRITTEN IN YOUR
OWN LANGUAGE. AND AS
YOU DO, TOUCH THE VELVET
DIRT, MOIST WITH THE
BLOOD OF GOD. HE DID
ALL OF THIS FOR YOU.

December 22

*The Lord is compassionate
and merciful.*

JAMES 5:11 NRSV

January 11

It is he who saved us and chose us for his holy work, not because we
deserved it but because that was his plan long before the world
began—to show his love and kindness to us through Christ. And
now he has made all of this plain to us by the coming of our Savior
Jesus Christ, who broke the power of death and showed us the way
of everlasting life through trusting him.

2 TIMOTHY 1:9–10 TLB

December 21

GIVE UP YOUR SINS BEFORE
THEY INFECT YOU AND
YOUR BITTERNESS BEFORE IT
INCITES YOU, AND GIVE
GOD YOUR ANXIETY
BEFORE IT INHIBITS YOU.

*Trust in the Lord with all your
heart and lean not on your own
understanding; in all your ways
acknowledge him, and he will
make your paths straight.*

PROVERBS 3:5–6 NIV

January 12

WHY GIVE A FLOWER
   FRAGRANCE?
WHY GIVE FOOD ITS TASTE?
COULD IT BE
   HE LOVES TO SEE
THAT LOOK UPON
   YOUR FACE?

*Taste and see that the Lord
is good; blessed is the man
who takes refuge in him.*

PSALM 34:8 NIV

December 20

But now in Christ Jesus you who once were far off have been
brought near by the blood of Christ. For he is our peace; in his
flesh he has made both groups into one and has broken down the
dividing wall, that is, the hostility between us. He has abolished
the law with its commandments and ordinances, that he might
create in himself one new humanity in place of the two, thus
making peace, and might reconcile both groups to God in one body
through the cross, thus putting to death that hostility through it.

EPHESIANS 2:13–16 NRSV

If we give gifts to show our love, how much more would he? If we—speckled with foibles and greed—love to give gifts, how much more does God, pure and perfect God, enjoy giving gifts to us?

January 13

If you…know how to give good gifts to your children, how much more will your heavenly Father give good gifts to those who ask him?

Matthew 7:11 nlt

December 19

Do you really want to keep a list? Do you really want to catalog all your mistreatments? Do you really want to growl and snap your way through life? God doesn't want you to either.

Love is patient, love is kind. It does not envy, it does not boast, it is not proud. It is not rude, it is not self-seeking, it is not easily angered.

1 CORINTHIANS 13:4 NIV

January 14

If we walk in the light, as he is in the light, we have fellowship with one another, and the blood of Jesus, his Son, purifies us from all sin.... If we confess our sins, he is faithful and just and will forgive us our sins and purify us from all unrighteousness.

1 John 1:7.9 NIV

December 18

Not easy. God wants us to leave our record of others' wrongs at the cross. "Just look what they did to me!" We defy and point to our hurts. "Just look what I did for you," he reminds and points to the cross. You and I are commanded—not urged, commanded—to keep no list of wrongs.

If someone does wrong to you, forgive that person because the Lord forgave you.

COLOSSIANS 3:13 NCV

January 15

Who is a God like you, who pardons sin and forgives the transgression of the remnant of his inheritance? You do not stay angry forever but delight to show mercy. You will again have compassion on us; you will tread our sins underfoot and hurl all our iniquities into the depths of the sea.

<small>MICAH 7:18–19 NIV</small>

December 17

We tend to fight back.
To keep lists and snarl
lips and growl at
people we don't like.
God wants your list.
He wants you to leave
the list at the cross.

Love keeps no

score of wrongs.

1 Corinthians 13:5 TEV

January 16

GOD'S GIFTS SHED LIGHT
ON GOD'S HEART, GOD'S
GOOD AND GENEROUS
HEART.

*Every desirable and beneficial
gift comes out of heaven. The
gifts are rivers of light cascading
down from the Father of Light.*

JAMES 1:17 MSG

December 16

He not only wants the mistakes we've made. He wants the ones we are making! Are you making some? If so, don't pretend nothing is wrong. Don't pretend you don't fall. Don't try to get back in the game. Go first to God. The first step after a stumble must be in the direction of the cross.

If we confess our sins to God, he can always be trusted to forgive us and take our sins away.

1 John 1:9 cev

EVERY GIFT REVEALS GOD'S
LOVE...BUT NO GIFT
REVEALS HIS LOVE MORE
THAN THE GIFTS OF THE
CROSS. THEY CAME, NOT
WRAPPED IN PAPER, BUT IN
PASSION. NOT PLACED
AROUND A TREE, BUT A
CROSS. AND NOT COVERED
WITH RIBBONS, BUT
SPRINKLED WITH BLOOD.

January 17

*The wages of sin is death; but
the gift of God is eternal life
through Jesus Christ Our Lord.*

ROMANS 6:23 KJV

December 15

You know that you were ransomed from the futile ways inherited from your ancestors, not with perishable things like silver or gold, but with the precious blood of Christ, like that of a lamb without defect or blemish. He was destined before the foundation of the world, but was revealed at the end of the ages for your sake. Through him you have come to trust in God, who raised him from the dead and gave him glory, so that your faith and hope are set on God.

1 PETER 1:18–21 NRSV

January 18

God has reserved for his children the priceless gift of eternal life; it is

kept in heaven for you, pure and undefiled, beyond the reach of

change and decay. And God, in his mighty power, will make sure that

you get there safely to receive it, because you are trusting him. It will

be yours in that coming last day for all to see.

1 PETER 1:4–5 TLB

December 14

GOD DOES MORE THAN
FORGIVE OUR MISTAKES;
HE REMOVES THEM! WE
SIMPLY HAVE TO TAKE
THEM TO HIM.

*This is my commitment to my
people: removal of their sins.*

ROMANS 11:27 MSG

MUCH HAS BEEN SAID ABOUT THE GIFT OF THE CROSS ITSELF, BUT WHAT OF THE OTHER GIFTS? WHAT OF THE NAILS, THE CROWN OF THORNS? THE GARMENTS TAKEN BY THE SOLDIERS. THE GARMENTS GIVEN FOR THE BURIAL. HAVE YOU TAKEN TIME TO OPEN THESE GIFTS? DIVINE GIFTS INTENDED TO STIR THAT MOMENT, THAT SPLIT SECOND WHEN YOUR FACE WILL BRIGHTEN, YOUR EYES WILL WIDEN, AND GOD WILL HEAR YOU WHISPER, "YOU DID THIS FOR ME?"

January 19

Thanks be to God for his
indescribable gift!
2 CORINTHIANS 9:15 NIV

December 13

You've seen what Christ left. Won't you leave something as well? Why don't you start with your bad moments? Your selfish moods and white lies? Give them to God. Your binges and bigotries? God wants them all. Every flop, every failure. He wants every single one. Why? Because he knows we can't live with them.

Let us throw off everything

that hinders and the sin

that so easily entangles.

HEBREWS 12:1 NIV

January 20

Your attitude should be the same as that of Christ Jesus: Who, being in very nature God, did not consider equality with God something to be grasped, but made himself nothing, taking the very nature of a servant, being made in human likeness. And being found in appearance as a man, he humbled himself and became obedient to death—even death on a cross! Therefore God exalted him to the highest place and gave him the name that is above every name, that at the man of Jesus every knee should bow, in heaven and on earth.

PHILIPPIANS 2:5–10 NIV

December 12

You can observe the cross and analyze the cross. You can read about it, even pray to it. But until you leave something there, you haven't embraced the cross.

Let us fix our eyes on Jesus, the author and perfecter of our faith, who for the joy set before him endured the cross, scorning its shame, and sat down at the right hand of the throne of God.

HEBREWS 12:2 NIV

THE DIADEM OF PAIN
WHICH SLICED YOUR GENTLE FACE,
THREE SPIKES PIERCING FLESH AND WOOD
TO HOLD YOU IN YOUR PLACE.
THE NEED FOR BLOOD I UNDERSTAND.
YOUR SACRIFICE I EMBRACE.
BUT THE BITTER SPONGE, THE CUTTING SPEAR,
THE SPIT UPON YOUR FACE?
DID IT HAVE TO BE A CROSS?

December 11

We have seen what Jesus brought to the cross. With scarred hands he offered forgiveness. Through torn skin he promised acceptance. He took the path to take us home. He wore our garment to give us his own. We have seen the gifts he brought. Now we ask, what will we bring?

Cast all your anxiety on him because he cares for you.

1 Peter 5:7 NIV

January 22

Did not a kinder death exist
than six hours hanging between life and death,
all spurred by a betrayer's kiss?
"Oh, Father," you pose,
heart-stilled at what could be,
"I'm sorry to ask, but I long to know,
did you do this for me?"

December 10

Jesus…looked toward heaven and prayed: "Father, the time
has come. Glorify your Son, that your Son may glorify
you. For you granted him authority over all people that he
might give eternal life to all those you have given him.
Now this is eternal life: that they may know you, the only
true God, and Jesus Christ, whom you have sent.

JOHN 17:1–3 NIV

January 23

Could it be that the hill of the cross is rich with God's gifts? Let's unwrap these gifts of grace as if for the first time. And as you touch them—as you feel the timber of the cross and trace the braid of the crown and finger the point of the spike—pause and listen. Perchance you will hear him whisper: "I did it just for you."

December 9

IN ORDER FOR THE CROSS OF CHRIST TO BE THE CROSS OF YOUR LIFE, YOU AND I NEED TO BRING SOMETHING TO THE HILL.

May I never boast except in the cross of our Lord Jesus Christ, through which the world has been crucified to me, and I to the world.

GALATIANS 6:14 NIV

January 24

The stripes that He bore and the thorns that He wore
 Told His mercy and love evermore;
And my heart bowed in shame as I called on His name,
 Calvary covers it all.
How matchless the grace, when I looked on the face
 Of this Jesus, my crucified Lord;
My redemption complete I then found at His feet,
 Calvary covers it all.

Mrs. Walter G. Taylor

WE WOULD HAVE SCRIPTED THE MOMENT DIFFERENTLY. ASK US HOW A GOD SHOULD REDEEM HIS WORLD, AND WE WILL SHOW YOU! WHITE HORSES, FLASHING SWORDS. EVIL FLAT ON HIS BACK. GOD ON HIS THRONE. BUT GOD ON A CROSS? NO, WE WOULDN'T HAVE WRITTEN THE DRAMA OF REDEMPTION THIS WAY. BUT, THEN AGAIN, WE WEREN'T ASKED TO. THESE PLAYERS AND PROPS WERE HEAVEN PICKED AND GOD ORDAINED.

December 8

But when the fullness of time had come, God sent his Son, born of a woman, born under the law.

GALATIANS 4:4 NRSV

January 25

Since all have sinned and fall short of the glory of God; they are now justified by his grace as a gift, through the redemption that is in Christ Jesus, whom God put forward as a sacrifice of atonement by his blood, effective through faith. He did this to show his righteousness, because in his divine forbearance he had passed over the sins previously committed; it was to prove at the present time that he himself is righteous and that he justifies the one who has faith in Jesus.

ROMANS 3:23–26 NRSV

As he gave his final breath, the earth gave a sudden stir. A rock rolled, and a soldier stumbled. Then, suddenly as the silence was broken, the silence returned. And now all is quiet. The mocking has ceased, There is no one to mock. And we are left with the relics of his death. Three nails in a bin. Three cross-shaped shadows. A braided crown with scarlet tips. Bizarre, isn't it? The thought that this blood is not man's blood but God's? Crazy, isn't it? Absurdities and ironies. The hill of Calvary is nothing if not both.

December 7

Then Jesus gave a loud cry and breathed his last.

MARK 15:37 NRSV

January 26

GOD'S PROMISE IN THE
SOLDIER'S SPIT:
I WILL BEAR YOUR
DARK SIDE.

*Then the soldiers bowed before
Jesus and made fun of him,
saying, "Hail, King of the
Jews!" They spat on Jesus. Then
they took his stick and began to
beat him on the head.*

MATTHEW 27:29–31 NCV

December 6

"My God! Why have you forsaken me?" He'd shouted a question to the heavens, and you half expected heaven to shout one in return. And apparently it did. For the face of Jesus softened, and an afternoon dawn broke as he spoke a final time. "It is finished. Father, into your hands I commit my spirit."

And at the ninth hour Jesus cried with a loud voice, saying, Eloi, Eloi, lama sabachthani? which is, being interpreted, My God, my God, why hast thou forsaken me?

MARK 15:34 KJV

January 27

Were you a slave when you were called? Don't let it trouble you—
although if you can gain your freedom, do so. For he who was a slave
when he was called by the Lord is the Lord's freedman; similarly, he
who was a free man when he was called is Christ's slave. You were
bought at a price; do not become slaves of men.

1 CORINTHIANS 7:21–23 NIV

December 5

How precious is your steadfast love, O God! All people may take

refuge in the shadow of your wings. They feast on the abundance of

your house, and you give them drink from the river of your delights.

For with you is the fountain of life; in your light we see light.

PSALM 36:7-9 NRSV

THE SOLDIERS' ASSIGNMENT WAS SIMPLE: TAKE THE NAZARENE TO THE HILL AND KILL HIM. BUT THEY HAD ANOTHER IDEA. THEY WANTED TO HAVE SOME FUN FIRST. STRONG, RESTED, ARMED SOLDIERS ENCIRCLED AN EXHAUSTED, NEARLY DEAD, GALILEAN CARPENTER AND BEAT UP ON HIM. THE SCOURGING WAS COMMANDED. THE CRUCIFIXION WAS ORDERED. BUT WHO WOULD DRAW PLEASURE OUT OF SPITTING ON A HALF-DEAD MAN?

January 28

They encourage each other in evil plans…. Surely the mind and heart of man are cunning.

PSALM 64:5–6 NIV

December 4

You yourself in your own conscience must feel Christ himself. You must experience unshakably that it is God's Word, even though the whole world should dispute it. As long as you do not have this feeling, you have certainly not yet tasted of God's Word.

MARTIN LUTHER

Heaven and earth will pass away, but my words will never pass away.

LUKE 21:33 NIV

January 29

SPITTING ISN'T INTENDED
TO HURT THE BODY—
IT CAN'T. SPITTING IS
INTENDED TO DEGRADE
THE SOUL, AND IT DOES.

[The soldiers] spit on him, and
took the staff and struck him on
the head again and again.

MATTHEW 27:30 NIV

December 3

No one can well perceive the power of faith unless he feels it by experience in his heart.

JOHN CALVIN

*This is the confidence we
have in approaching God:
that if we ask anything
according to his will, he hears us.*

1 JOHN 5:14 NIV

January 30

So when Pilate saw that he could do nothing, but rather that a riot was beginning, he took some water and washed his hands before the crowd, saying, "I am innocent of this man's blood; see to it yourselves." Then the people as a whole answered, "His blood be on us and on our children!" So he released Barabbas for them; and after flogging Jesus, he handed him over to be crucified.

MATTHEW 27:24–26 NRSV

December 2

THE WORDS OF KING
HEROD WHEN TOLD OF THE
BIRTH OF JESUS: "KILL HIM.
THERE IS ROOM FOR ONLY
ONE KING IN THIS CORNER
OF THE WORLD." THE
VERDICT AFTER TWO
MILLENNIUMS: HEROD WAS
RIGHT...THERE IS ROOM
FOR ONLY ONE KING.

*Jesus Christ…is the faithful
witness, the firstborn from
the dead, and the ruler of
the kings of the earth.*

REVELATION 1:5 NIV

January 31

WHAT WERE THE SOLDIERS DOING? WERE THEY NOT ELEVATING THEMSELVES AT THE EXPENSE OF ANOTHER? THEY FELT BIG BY MAKING CHRIST LOOK SMALL.

And they began to call out to him, "Hail, king of the Jews!" Again and again they struck him on the head with a staff and spit on him. Falling on their knees, they paid homage to him. And when they had mocked him...they led him out to crucify him.

MARK 15:18–20 NIV

December 1

THE REASON JESUS DIED
AND ROSE AGAIN:
THE FACE IN YOUR MIRROR.

Christ loved us and gave
himself up for us as a fragrant
offering and sacrifice to God.

EPHESIANS 5:2 NIV

February 1

Sin, understood in the Christian sense, is the rent which cuts through the whole of existence.

Emil Brunner

The heart is deceitful above all things and beyond cure. Who can understand it?

Jeremiah 17:9 niv

November 30

I will praise you, O Lord, among the nations; I will sing of you

among the peoples. For great is your love, reaching to the heavens;

your faithfulness reaches to the skies. Be exalted, O God,

above the heavens; let your glory be over all the earth.

<small>PSALMS 57:9-11 NIV</small>

February 2

Have you ever raised your hand in anger or rolled your eyes in arrogance? Have you ever blasted your high beams in someone's rearview mirror? Ever made someone feel bad so you would feel good? How we treat others is how we treat Jesus.

I assure you, when you did it to one of the least of these my brothers and sisters, you were doing it to me!

Matthew 25:40 NLT

November 29

When he died, so did your sin. And when he rose, so did your hope. For when he rose, your grave was changed from a final residence to temporary housing.

But thanks be to God, who always leads us in victory through Christ.

2 Corinthians 2:14 NCV

February 3

Have you ever surprised yourself? Have you ever reflected on an act and wondered, "What got into me?" The Bible has a three-letter answer for that question: S-I-N. There is something bad—beastly—within each of us. It is not that we can't do good. We do. It's just that we can't keep from doing bad. Though made in God's image, we have fallen.

All we like sheep have gone astray; We have turned, every one, to his own way.

Isaiah 53:6 NKJV

JESUS WAS A BACKWATER
PEASANT. HE NEVER
WROTE A BOOK, NEVER
HELD AN OFFICE. HE NEVER
JOURNEYED MORE THAN
TWO HUNDRED MILES FROM
HIS HOMETOWN. FRIENDS
LEFT HIM. ONE BETRAYED
HIM. THOSE HE HELPED
FORGOT HIM. PRIOR TO HIS
DEATH THEY ABANDONED
HIM. BUT AFTER HIS DEATH
THEY COULDN'T RESIST
HIM. WHAT MADE THE
DIFFERENCE? HIS DEATH
AND RESURRECTION.

November 28

*If you confess with your
mouth, "Jesus is Lord,"
and believe in your heart that
God raised him from the dead,
you will be saved.*

ROMANS 10:9 NIV

February 4

"Compared to everyone else, I'm a decent person." You know, a pig might say something similar. He might look at his trough partners and announce, "I'm just as clean as everyone else." Compared to humans, however, that pig needs help. Compared to God, we humans need the same. The standard for sinlessness isn't found at the pig troughs of earth but at the throne of heaven. God, himself, is the standard.

As he who called you is holy,
so be holy in all you do.
1 Peter 1:15 NIV

THE MOVEMENT CONTINUES

The facts: Christianity has never been stronger. Over one billion Catholics and nearly as many Protestants.

November 27

This gospel of the kingdom will be preached in the whole world as a testimony to all nations, and then the end will come.

MATTHEW 24:14 NIV

February 5

For we know that our old self was crucified with him so that the body of sin might be done away with, that we should no longer be slaves to sin—because anyone who has died has been freed from sin. Now if we died with Christ, we believe that we will also live with him.

ROMANS 6:6–8 NIV

THE MOVEMENT CONTINUES

THE DISCOVERY MADE BY EVERY PERSON WHO HAS TRIED TO BURY THE FAITH: THE SAME AS THE ONE MADE BY THOSE WHO TRIED TO BURY ITS FOUNDER. HE WON'T STAY IN THE TOMB.

November 26

Why do you look for the living among the ~~dead~~?

He is not here; '~~ ~~

LUKE ~~2~~

February 6

"THERE IS NO MAN SO GOOD, WHO, WERE HE TO SUBMIT ALL HIS THOUGHTS AND ACTIONS TO THE LAWS, WOULD NOT DESERVE HANGING TEN TIMES IN HIS LIFE."

MICHEL DE MONTAIGNE

For God did not send his Son into the world to condemn the world, but to save the world through him.

JOHN 3:17 NIV

November 25

He is not here. He was raised, just as he said. Come and

look at the place where he was placed. Now, get on your

way quickly and tell his disciples, "He is risen from the dead."

MATTHEW 28:6-7 MSG

February 7

The soldiers led Jesus away into the palace (that is, the Praetorium) and called together the whole company of soldiers. They put a purple robe on him, then twisted together a crown of thorns and set it on him. And they began to call out to him, "Hail, king of the Jews!"

MARK 15:16–18 NIV

THE MOVEMENT CONTINUES

The pronouncement of Friedrich Nietzsche in 1882: "God is dead." The dawn of science, he believed, would be the doom of faith. Science has dawned; the movement continues. The way a Communist dictionary defined the Bible: "It is a collection of fantastic legends without any scientific support." Communism is diminishing; the movement continues.

November 24

The fool says in his heart,

"There is no God."

Psalm 53:1 NIV

WE HAVE A PROBLEM: WE ARE NOT HOLY, AND
"ANYONE WHOSE LIFE IS NOT HOLY WILL NEVER SEE THE
LORD" (HEB. 12:14). WE HAVE A PROBLEM: WE ARE EVIL,
AND "EVIL PEOPLE ARE PAID WITH PUNISHMENT"
(PROV. 10:16). OBSERVE WHAT JESUS DOES WITH OUR FILTH.
HE CARRIES IT TO THE CROSS.

THE MOVEMENT CONTINUES

The belief of French philosopher Voltaire: The Bible and Christianity would pass within a hundred years. He died in 1778. The movement continues.

November 23

Surely I am with you always, to the very end of the age.

MATTHEW 28:20 NIV

I DID NOT HIDE MY FACE FROM THE MOCKING AND SPITTING (ISA. 50:6). MINGLED WITH HIS BLOOD AND SWEAT WAS THE ESSENCE OF OUR SIN. IN GOD'S PLAN, JESUS WAS OFFERED WINE FOR HIS THROAT, SO WHY NOT A TOWEL FOR HIS FACE?

February 9

I gave my back to those who struck me, and my cheeks to those who pulled out the beard; I did not hide my face from insult and spitting.

ISAIAH 50:6 NRSV

HIS MOVEMENT

The official response of the Jewish leaders to the conversion of Saul: Good riddance to the former Pharisee. Won't be months before he is in jail, and then what will he do? Write letters? What Saul, turned Paul, understood that his former colleagues didn't: Salvation is found in no one else.

November 22

God gave [Jesus] as a way to forgive sin.

ROMANS 3:25 NCV

SIMON CARRIED THE CROSS
OF JESUS, BUT HE DIDN'T
MOP THE CHEEK OF JESUS.
ANGELS WERE A PRAYER
AWAY. COULDN'T THEY
HAVE TAKEN THE SPITTLE
AWAY? THEY COULD
HAVE, BUT JESUS NEVER
COMMANDED THEM TO.
FOR SOME REASON, THE
ONE WHO CHOSE THE NAILS
ALSO CHOSE THE SALIVA.
ALONG WITH THE SPEAR
AND THE SPONGE OF MAN,
HE BORE THE SPIT OF MAN.

February 10

When he was abused,
he did not return abuse;
when he suffered, he himself
did not threaten; but he
entrusted himself to the
one who judges justly.
1 PETER 2:24 NRSV

HIS MOVEMENT

THE DECISION OF THE
JEWISH LEADERS ABOUT THE
CHURCH: "IF THEIR PLAN
COMES FROM HUMAN
AUTHORITY, IT WILL FAIL.
BUT IF IT IS FROM GOD, YOU
WILL NOT BE ABLE TO STOP
THEM" (ACTS 5:38–39).
THE RESPONSE OF THE
CHURCH: GROWTH.

November 21

*The number of
followers was growing.*

ACTS 6:1 NCV

God is light and in him there is no darkness at all. If we say
that we have fellowship with him while we are walking in darkness,
we lie and do not do what is true; but if we walk in the light
as he himself is in the light, we have fellowship with one another,
and the blood of Jesus his Son cleanses us from all sin....
If we confess our sins, he who is faithful and just will forgive
us our sins and cleanse us from all unrighteousness.

1 JOHN 1:5–7,9 NRSV

November 20

It was fitting that God, for whom and through whom all things

exist, in bringing many children to glory, should make the pioneer

of their salvation perfect through sufferings. For the one who

sanctifies and those who are sanctified all have one Father.

HEBREWS 2:10–11 NRSV

February 12

GOD'S PROMISE IN THE
CROWN OF THORNS:
I LOVED YOU ENOUGH
TO BECOME ONE
OF YOU.

*They took off his clothes and
put a red robe on him. Using
thorny branches, they made a
crown, put it on his head, and
put a stick in his right hand.*

MATTHEW 27:28–29 NCV

HIS MOVEMENT

The official response of the Jewish leaders to the rumors of the resurrection: Of course they say he's alive. They have to. What else can they say? The actual response of the Jewish leaders to the resurrection of Jesus: They believed.

A great number of the Jewish priests believed and obeyed.

Acts 6:7 NCV

November 19

February 13

SCRIPTURE SAYS THAT THE NUMBER OF GOD'S YEARS IS UNSEARCHABLE. WE MAY SEARCH OUT THE MOMENT THE FIRST WAVE SLAPPED ON A SHORE OR THE FIRST STAR BURST IN THE SKY, BUT WE'LL NEVER FIND THE FIRST MOMENT WHEN GOD WAS GOD, FOR THERE IS NO MOMENT WHEN GOD WAS NOT GOD. HE HAS NEVER NOT BEEN, FOR HE IS ETERNAL. GOD IS NOT BOUND BY TIME.

Surely God is great…
the number of his years
is unsearchable.

JOB 36:26 NRSV

HIS EXECUTION

The odds a street-corner bookie would've given the day after the crucifixion on the possibility that Jesus' name would be known in the year 2000: "I'll give you better odds that he'll rise from the dead."

So they went and made the tomb secure by putting a seal on the stone and posting the guard.

Matthew 27:66 NIV

November 18

OUR ASKING "WHERE IS GOD?" IS LIKE A FISH ASKING "WHERE IS WATER?" OR A BIRD ASKING "WHERE IS AIR?" GOD IS EVERYWHERE! EQUALLY PRESENT IN PEKING AND PEORIA. AS ACTIVE IN THE LIVES OF ICELANDERS AS IN THE LIVES OF TEXANS. WE CANNOT FIND A PLACE WHERE GOD IS NOT.

February 14

He shall have dominion
also from sea to sea,
And from the River to the
ends of the earth.

PSALM 72:8 NKJV

November 17

Alas! And did my Savior bleed?
  And did my Sov'reign die?
Would He devote that sacred head
  For sinners such as I!
Was it for crimes that I have done
  He groaned upon the tree?
Amazing pity! Grace unknown!
  And love beyond degree!

Isaac Watts

WHEN GOD ENTERED TIME
AND BECAME A MAN, HE
WHO WAS BOUNDLESS
BECAME BOUND. IMPRISONED
IN FLESH. RESTRICTED BY
WEARY-PRONE MUSCLES
AND EYELIDS. FOR MORE
THAN THREE DECADES, HIS
ONCE LIMITLESS REACH
WOULD BE LIMITED TO THE
STRETCH OF AN ARM, HIS
SPEED CHECKED TO THE
PACE OF HUMAN FEET. I
WONDER, WAS HE EVER
TEMPTED TO RECLAIM HIS
BOUNDLESSNESS?

February 15

Jesus…made himself nothing,
taking the very nature of a
servant, being made in
human likeness.

PHILIPPIANS 2:4, 7 NIV

HIS EXECUTION

THE NUMBER OF TIMES JESUS PROPHESIED THAT HE WOULD COME BACK TO LIFE THREE DAYS AFTER HIS DEATH: THREE. THE NUMBER OF APOSTLES WHO HEARD THE PROPHECY: ALL OF THEM. THE NUMBER OF APOSTLES WHO WAITED AT THE TOMB TO SEE IF HE WOULD DO WHAT HE SAID: ZERO.

November 16

Destroy this temple, and I will raise it again in three days.

JOHN 2:19 NIV

February 16

And Christ became a human being and lived here on earth among us and was full of loving forgiveness and truth. And some of us have seen his glory—the glory of the only Son of the heavenly Father!

JOHN 1:14 TLB

November 15

Praise be to the God and Father of our Lord Jesus Christ! In his
great mercy he has given us new birth into a living hope through
the resurrection of Jesus Christ from the dead, and into an
inheritance that can never perish, spoil or fade—in heaven for you,
who through faith are shielded by God's power until the coming
of the salvation that is ready to be revealed in the last time.

1 PETER 1:3-5 NIV

February 17

He not only perfectly understands our case and our problem, but He has morally, actively, finally solved it.

P. T. Forsyth

For God so loved the world that he gave his one and only Son, that whoever believes in him shall not perish but have eternal life.

John 3:16 niv

HIS EXECUTION

THE POPULAR OPINION REGARDING JESUS BEFORE HE CLEANSED THE TEMPLE: SEE IF HE'LL RUN FOR OFFICE. THE POPULAR OPINION REGARDING JESUS AFTER HE CLEANSED THE TEMPLE: LET'S SEE HOW FAST HE CAN RUN.

November 14

So he made a whip out of cords, and drove all from the temple area.... Then the Jews demanded of him, "What miraculous sign can you show us to prove your authority to do all this?"

JOHN 2:15,18 NIV

February 18

*Therefore, there is now no condemnation for those who are in
Christ Jesus, because through Christ Jesus the law of the
Spirit of life set me free from the law of sin and death. For
what the law was powerless to do in that it was weakened
by the sinful nature, God did by sending his own Son in
the likeness of sinful man to be a sin offering.*

ROMANS 8:1–3 NIV

HIS MINISTRY

The number of lepers and blind and lame people Jesus healed: Too many to count. The number of healed lepers and blind and lame people who defended Jesus on the day of his death: Zero.

November 13

Many followed him,
and he healed all their sick.

MATTHEW 12:15 NIV

February 19

In the middle of a long trip, did Jesus ever consider transporting himself to the next city? When the rain chilled his bones, was he tempted to change the weather? Stop and think about this. Not once did Christ use his supernatural powers for personal comfort.

Father, if you are willing, take this cup from me; yet not my will, but yours be done.

LUKE 22:42 NIV

HIS MINISTRY

THE NUMBER OF DISCIPLES JESUS RECRUITED: SEVENTY. THE NUMBER OF DISCIPLES WHO DEFENDED HIM TO THE AUTHORITIES: ZERO. THE ASSESSMENT OF JESUS' FOLLOWERS AS FOUND IN THE JERUSALEM EDITORIAL PAGE: A GROUP OF UNEMPLOYED NE'ER-DO-WELLS RECRUITED OFF THE SHIPPING DOCKS AND OUT OF THE RED-LIGHT DISTRICTS.

November 12

Then all the disciples deserted him and left.

MATTHEW 26:56 NIV

February 20

WITH ONE WORD HE COULD'VE TRANSFORMED THE HARD EARTH INTO A SOFT BED, BUT HE DIDN'T. WITH A WAVE OF HIS HAND, HE COULD'VE BOOMERANGED THE SPIT OF HIS ACCUSERS BACK INTO THEIR FACES, BUT HE DIDN'T. WITH AN ARCH OF HIS BROW, HE COULD'VE PARALYZED THE HAND OF THE SOLDIER AS HE BRAIDED THE CROWN OF THORNS. BUT HE DIDN'T.

Who, being in very nature God, did not consider equality with God something to be grasped, but made himself nothing.

PHILIPPIANS 2:6–7 NIV

HIS BIRTH
THE REWARD GIVEN TO
JOSEPH AND MARY FOR
BRINGING GOD INTO THE
WORLD: TWO YEARS IN
EXILE, LEARNING
EGYPTIAN. THIS WAS THE
BEGINNING OF THE
CHRISTIAN MOVEMENT.
(AND THESE WERE THE
CALM YEARS.)

November 11

*An angel of the Lord appeared
to Joseph in a dream. "Get up,"
he said, "take the child and his
mother and escape to
Egypt…for Herod is going to
search for the child to kill him."*

MATTHEW 2:13 NIV

February 21

Now in Christ Jesus, you who were far away from God are brought near through the blood of Christ's death. Christ himself is our peace.... Christ came and preached peace to you who were far away from God, and to those who were near to God. Yes, it is through Christ we all have the right to come to the Father in one Spirit.

EPHESIANS 2:13–14, 17–18 NCV

November 10

For we know that since Christ was raised from the dead,

he cannot die again; death no longer has mastery over him. The

death he died, he died to sin once for all; but the life he lives,

he lives to God. In the same way, count yourselves

dead to sin but alive to God in Christ Jesus.

ROMANS 6:9–11 NIV

THE MOST REMARKABLE PART OF JESUS' COMING WAS HIS SURRENDER OF SINLESSNESS. ISN'T THIS THE MESSAGE OF THE CROWN OF THORNS? THROUGHOUT SCRIPTURE THORNS SYMBOLIZE, NOT SIN, BUT THE CONSEQUENCE OF SIN. THE FRUIT OF SIN IS THORNS—SPINY, PRICKLY, CUTTING THORNS.

February 22

God made him who had no sin to be sin for us, so that in him we might become the righteousness of God.

2 CORINTHIANS 5:21 NIV

November 9

HIS BIRTH

THE NUMBER OF RELIGIOUS LEADERS WHO BELIEVED A MESSIAH HAD BEEN BORN IN BETHLEHEM: ZERO. THE TYPE OF PEOPLE WHO DID: SOME STARGAZERS, NIGHT-SHIFT SHEPHERDS, AND A COUPLE OF NEWLYWEDS WHO CLAIMED TO HAVE MORE EXPERIENCE GIVING BIRTH THAN HAVING SEX.

We saw his star in the east and have come to worship him.

MATTHEW 2:2 NIV

February 23

IF THE FRUIT OF SIN IS
THORNY CROWN ON
CHRIST'S BROW A PICTURE
OF THE FRUIT OF OUR SIN
THAT PIERCED HIS HEART?

Surely he hath borne our griefs,
And carried our sorrows:
Yet we did esteem Him stricken,
Smitten of God, and afflicted.

ISAIAH 53:4 KJV

ON THE FIRST EASTER
MORNING...THE SMOTHERING
SILENCE THAT INSULATES THE
DOMAIN OF THE DEAD FROM
THE WORLD OF THE LIVING
WAS SUDDENLY SHATTERED.

GILBERT BILEZIKIAN

With the cross,

[God] won the victory.

COLOSSIANS 2:15 NCV

February 24

THE ONE WHO PLAYED
MARBLES WITH THE STARS
GAVE IT UP TO PLAY
MARBLES WITH MARBLES.

When I consider your heavens,

the work of your fingers,

the moon and the stars,

which you have set in place,

what is man that you are

mindful of him, the son of man

that you care for him?

PSALM 8:3–4 NIV

November 7

GOD'S PROMISE
IN THE EMPTY TOMB:
I HAVE WON
THE VICTORY.

*In the resurrection scheme of things, this
has to happen: everything perishable
taken off the shelves and replaced by
the imperishable, this mortal replaced
by the immortal.... But now in a
single victorious stroke of Life, all three—
sin, guilt, death—are gone, the gift of
our Master, Jesus Christ. Thank God!*

1 CORINTHIANS 15:54,57 MSG

February 25

THE ONE WHO HUNG THE
GALAXIES GAVE IT UP TO
HANG DOORJAMBS TO THE
DISPLEASURE OF A CRANKY
CLIENT WHO WANTED
EVERYTHING YESTERDAY
BUT COULDN'T PAY
FOR ANYTHING UNTIL
TOMORROW.

*He who made the Pleiades and
Orion, who turns blackness into
dawn…the Lord is his name.*

AMOS 5:8 NIV

As hard as it may be to believe, you could be only a Saturday away from a resurrection. You could be only hours from that precious prayer of a changed heart, "God, did you do this for me?"

And the God of all grace, who called you to his eternal glory in Christ, after you have suffered a little while, will himself restore you and make you strong, firm and steadfast.

1 Peter 5:10 NIV

November 6

February 26

When Christ came as high priest of the good things that are already here, he went through the greater and more perfect tabernacle that is not man-made, that is to say, not a part of this creation. He did not enter by means of the blood of goats and calves; but he entered the Most Holy Place once for all by his own blood, having obtained eternal redemption.

HEBREWS 9:11–12 NIV

November 5

He has rescued us from the power of darkness and transferred us into the kingdom of his beloved Son, in whom we have redemption, the forgiveness of sins. He is the image of the invisible God, the firstborn of all creation; for in him all things in heaven and on earth were created, things visible and invisible, whether thrones or dominions or rulers or powers—all things have been created through him and for him.

COLOSSIANS 1:13–16 NRSV

February 27

JESUS, IN AN INSTANT, WENT FROM NEEDING NOTHING TO NEEDING AIR, FOOD, A TUB OF HOT WATER AND SALTS FOR HIS TIRED FEET, AND, MORE THAN ANYTHING, NEEDING SOMEBODY— ANYBODY—WHO WAS MORE CONCERNED ABOUT WHERE HE WOULD SPEND ETERNITY THAN WHERE HE WOULD SPEND FRIDAY'S PAYCHECK.

You were bought, not with something that ruins like gold or silver, but with the precious blood of Christ, who was like a pure and perfect lamb. Christ was chosen before the world was made.

1 PETER 1:18–20 NCV

THE BIBLE SAYS THAT "IN
EVERYTHING GOD WORKS FOR
THE GOOD OF THOSE WHO LOVE
HIM." REMOVE THE WORD
EVERYTHING, AND REPLACE IT
WITH THE SYMBOL OF YOUR
TRAGEDY. HOW WOULD
ROMANS 8:28 READ IN YOUR
LIFE? IN HOSPITAL STAYS GOD
WORKS FOR THE GOOD. IN
DIVORCE PAPERS GOD WORKS
FOR THE GOOD. IN A PRISON
TERM GOD WORKS FOR THE
GOOD. IF GOD CAN CHANGE
JOHN'S LIFE THROUGH A
TRAGEDY, COULD IT BE HE
WILL USE A TRAGEDY TO
CHANGE YOURS?

November 4

*That's why we can be so sure
that every detail in our lives
of love for God is worked
into something good.*

ROMANS 8:28 MSG

He gave no command to the angels who begged, "Just give the nod, Lord. One word and these demons will be deviled eggs." He refused to defend himself when blamed for every sin of every slut and sailor since Adam. He stood silent as a million guilty verdicts echoed in the tribunal of heaven and the giver of light was left in the chill of a sinner's night.

February 28

The Word became flesh and made his dwelling among us. We have seen his glory, the glory of the One and Only, who came from the Father, full of grace and truth.

John 1:14 NIV

November 3

"GOD WORKS FOR THE GOOD OF THOSE WHO LOVE HIM" (ROM. 8:28). THAT'S HOW JOHN FELT ABOUT JESUS. HE LOVED HIM. HE DIDN'T UNDERSTAND HIM OR ALWAYS AGREE WITH HIM, BUT HE LOVED HIM. AND BECAUSE HE LOVED HIM, HE STAYED NEAR HIM.

Draw near to God, and he
will draw near to you.

JAMES 4:8 NRSV

February 29

Every good and perfect gift is from above, coming down from the

Father of the heavenly lights, who does not change like shifting

shadows. He chose to give us birth through the word of truth,

that we might be a kind of firstfruits of all he created.

James 1:17–18 NIV

November 2

In God's hand empty wine jugs at a wedding become a symbol of power. The coin of a widow becomes a symbol of generosity. A crude manger in Bethlehem is his symbol of devotion. And a tool of death is a symbol of his love. Should we be surprised that he takes the wrappings of death and makes them the picture of life?

For to this end Christ both died, and rose, and revived, that he might be Lord both of the dead and living.

ROMANS 14:9 KJV

AFTER THREE DAYS IN A
DARK HOLE JESUS STEPPED
INTO THE EASTER SUNRISE
WITH A SMILE AND A
SWAGGER AND A QUESTION
FOR LOWLY LUCIFER—"IS
THAT YOUR BEST PUNCH?"
THAT WAS COOL,
INCREDIBLY COOL. BUT
WANT TO KNOW THE
COOLEST THING ABOUT THE
ONE WHO GAVE UP THE
CROWN OF HEAVEN FOR
A CROWN OF THORNS?
HE DID IT FOR YOU.
JUST FOR YOU.

March 1

*For God did not send his Son
into the world to condemn the
world, but to save the world
through him.*

JOHN 3:17 NIV

THROUGH THE RAGS OF
DEATH, JOHN SAW THE
POWER OF LIFE. ODD,
DON'T YOU THINK,
THAT GOD WOULD
USE SOMETHING AS SAD
AS A BURIAL WRAP TO
CHANGE A LIFE? BUT
GOD IS GIVEN TO
SUCH PRACTICES.

November 1

He saw the linen wrappings lying
there, and the cloth that had been
on Jesus' head, not lying with
the linen wrappings but rolled
up in a place by itself. Then
the other disciple, who reached
the tomb first, also went in,
and he saw and believed.

JOHN 20:6–8 NRSV

March 2

Indeed, God did not send the Son into the world to condemn the
world, but in order that the world might be saved through him.
Those who believe in him are not condemned; but those who
do not believe are condemned already, because they have
not believed in the name of the only Son of God.

JOHN 3:17–18 NRSV

October 31

The women who had come with Jesus from Galilee followed

Joseph and saw the tomb and how his body was laid in it.

Then they went home and prepared spices and perfumes. But they

rested on the Sabbath in obedience to the commandment.

On the first day of the week, very early in the morning, the

women took the spices they had prepared and went to the tomb.

They found the stone rolled away from the tomb, but when

they entered, they did not find the body of the Lord Jesus.

<small>LUKE 23:55–24:3 NIV</small>

March 3

GOD'S PROMISE
IN THE NAILS:
I FORGIVE YOU.

He forgave all our sins. He
canceled the debt, which listed all
the rules we failed to follow. He
took away that record with its
rules and nailed it to the cross.

COLOSSIANS 2:13–14 NCV

October 30

IF FRIENDS HAD REMOVED THE BODY, WOULD THEY NOT HAVE TAKEN THE CLOTHES WITH IT? IF FOES HAD TAKEN THE BODY, WOULD THEY NOT HAVE DONE THE SAME? BUT IF NEITHER FRIEND NOR FOE TOOK THE BODY, WHO DID? THIS WAS JOHN'S QUESTION, AND THIS QUESTION LED TO JOHN'S DISCOVERY.

He saw and believed.

JOHN 20:8 NCV

HE NEVER SHOULD HAVE
ASKED ME TO KEEP THE LIST.
I DREAD SHOWING IT TO HIM.
HE'S A SKILLED BUILDER, A FINE
FRIEND. AND HE HAS BUILT US
A GREAT HOUSE. BUT THE
HOUSE HAS A FEW MISTAKES.
LOOKING AT THE LIST OF THE
BUILDER'S MISTAKES CAUSED
ME TO THINK ABOUT GOD
MAKING A LIST OF MINE.
AFTER ALL, HASN'T HE TAKEN
UP RESIDENCE IN MY HEART?
AND IF I SEE FLAWS IN MY
HOUSE, IMAGINE WHAT HE SEES
IN ME. OH, DARE WE THINK OF
THE LIST HE COULD COMPILE?

March 4

When you were dead in your
sins and in the uncircumcision
of your sinful nature, God
made you alive with Christ.
He forgave us all our sins.

COLOSSIANS 2:13 NIV

October 29

John chose to linger near Jesus. And because he lingered on Saturday, he was around on Sunday to see the miracle. Mary said, "They have taken the Lord out of the tomb, and we don't know where they have put him."

As they entered the tomb, they saw a young man dressed in a white robe sitting on the right side, and they were alarmed. "Don't be alarmed," he said. "You are looking for Jesus the Nazarene, who was crucified. He has risen! He is not here.

MARK 16:5-6 NIV

For all at once all sin is atoned for on the Cross, the entire Fall is erased, and the whole obligation to Satan and the entire sentence passed upon the Fall of Adam is torn up, cancelled, and annulled by the nails of Jesus.

COUNT NIKOLAUS LUDWIG
VON ZINZENDORF

March 5

Jesus of Nazareth…was handed over to you by God's set purpose and foreknowledge; and you…put him to death by nailing him to the cross. But God raised him from the dead.

ACTS 2:22–24 NIV

WHAT ABOUT YOU?
WHEN YOU'RE IN JOHN'S
POSITION, WHAT DO YOU
DO? WHEN IT'S SATURDAY
IN YOUR LIFE, HOW DO YOU
REACT? WHEN YOU ARE
SOMEWHERE BETWEEN
YESTERDAY'S TRAGEDY
AND TOMORROW'S
TRIUMPH, WHAT DO YOU
DO? DO YOU LEAVE
GOD—OR DO YOU LINGER
NEAR HIM?

October 28

Yet, O Lord, you are our
Father; we are the clay,
and you are our potter; we are
all the work of your hand.

ISAIAH 64:8 NRSV

The door hinges to the prayer room have grown rusty from underuse. The stove called jealousy is overheating. The attic floor is weighted with too many regrets. The cellar is cluttered with too many secrets. And won't someone raise the shutter and chase the pessimism out of this heart? The list of our weaknesses. Would you like anyone to see yours? Would you like them made public?

March 6

For we do not have a high priest who is unable to sympathize with our weakness.... Let us therefore approach the throne of grace with boldness, so that we may receive mercy and find grace to help in time of need.

HEBREWS 4:15–16 NRSV

October 27

JOHN HAD A HABIT OF
DOING THIS. HE WAS CLOSE
TO JESUS IN THE UPPER
ROOM. HE WAS CLOSE TO
JESUS IN THE GARDEN OF
GETHSEMANE. HE WAS AT
THE FOOT OF THE CROSS AT
THE CRUCIFIXION, AND HE
WAS A QUICK WALK FROM
THE TOMB AT THE BURIAL.
DID HE UNDERSTAND
JESUS? NO. WAS HE GLAD
JESUS DID WHAT HE DID?
NO. BUT DID HE LEAVE
JESUS? NO.

One of his disciples—
the one whom Jesus loved—
was reclining next to him.

JOHN 13:23 NRSV

March 7

When you were slaves of sin, you were free in regard to

righteousness. So what advantage did you then get from the

things of which you now are ashamed? The end of those

things is death. But now that you have been freed from

sin and enslaved to God, the advantage you get is sanctification.

The end is eternal life. For the wages of sin is death, but

the free gift of God is eternal life in Christ Jesus our Lord.

ROMANS 6:20–23 NRSV

October 26

Beloved, let us love one another, because love is from God;

everyone who loves is born of God and knows God.

Whoever does not love does not know God, for God is love.

God's love was revealed among us in this way: God sent

his only Son into the world so that we might live through him.

In this is love, not that we loved God but that he loved

us and sent his Son to be the atoning sacrifice for our sins.

1 JOHN 4:7–10 NRSV

March 8

Yes, there is a list of your failures. Christ has chronicled your shortcomings. And, yes, that list has been made public. But you've never seen it. Neither have I.

He canceled the record that contained the charges against us. He took it and destroyed it by nailing it to Christ's cross.

Colossians 2:14 nlt

October 25

To others, Jesus was a miracle worker. To others, Jesus was a master teacher. To others, Jesus was the hope of Israel. But to John, he was all of these and more. To John, Jesus was a friend. You don't abandon a friend—not even when that friend is dead. John stayed close to Jesus.

I have called you friends, because I have made known to you everything that I have heard from my Father.

JOHN 15:15 NRSV

March 9

Jesus turns his face toward the nail just as the soldier lifts the hammer to strike it. Couldn't Jesus have stopped him? With a flex of the biceps, with a clench of the fist, he could have resisted.

And as a sheep before its shearers is silent, so He opened not His mouth.

Isaiah 53:7 NKJV

JESUS WAS DEAD. THE
MASTER'S BODY WAS
LIFELESS. JOHN'S FRIEND
AND FUTURE WERE BURIED.
BUT JOHN HAD NOT LEFT.
WHY? WAS HE WAITING
FOR THE RESURRECTION?
NO. PERHAPS HE WAS
TAKING CARE OF JESUS'
MOTHER. OR PERHAPS HE
DIDN'T HAVE ANYWHERE
ELSE TO GO. COULD BE
HE DIDN'T HAVE ANY
MONEY OR ENERGY OR
DIRECTION.... OR MAYBE HE
LINGERED BECAUSE HE
LOVED JESUS.

October 24

*So she ran and went to Simon
Peter and the other disciple,
the one whom Jesus loved,
and said to them, "They have
taken the Lord out of the tomb,
and we do not know
where they have laid him."*

JOHN 20:2 NRSV

March 10

IS THIS NOT THE SAME HAND THAT STILLED THE SEA? CLEANSED THE TEMPLE? SUMMONED THE DEAD? HIS FIST DOESN'T CLENCH...AND THE MOMENT ISN'T ABORTED. WHY? WHY DIDN'T JESUS RESIST? BECAUSE HE LOVED US.

But God who is rich in mercy, because of His great love with which He loved us, even when we were dead in trespasses, made us alive together with Christ.

EPHESIANS 2:4-5 NKJV

October 23

What John did on Saturday is so important. We don't know anything about this day; we have no passage to read, no knowledge to share. All we know is this: When Sunday came, John was still present.

Watch and pray so that you will not fall into temptation.

Matthew 26:41 niv

JESUS TURNED HIS FACE
TOWARD THE NAIL AS
THE SOLDIER LIFTED THE
HAMMER TO STRIKE IT.
WITH HIS CHEEK RESTING
ON THE WOOD HE SAW THE
HAND OF GOD. IT APPEARED
TO BE THE HAND OF A MAN.
LONG FINGERS OF A
WOODWORKER. CALLOUS
PALMS OF A CARPENTER.
IT APPEARED COMMON.
IT WAS, HOWEVER,
ANYTHING BUT.

March 11

Filled with compassion,
Jesus reached out his hand
and touched the man....
Immediately the
leprosy left him.
MARK 1:41–42 NIV

October 22

Then [Jesus] took the cup, gave thanks and offered it to them saying, "Drink from it, all of you. This is my blood of the covenant, which is poured out for many for the forgiveness of sins. I tell you, I will not drink of this fruit of the vine from now on until that day when I drink it anew with you in my Father's kingdom."

MATTHEW 26:27–29 NIV

March 12

For all have sinned and fall short of the glory of God,

and are justified freely by his grace through the

redemption that came by Christ Jesus.

ROMANS 3:23–24 NIV

October 21

JOHN DIDN'T KNOW
ON THAT FRIDAY WHAT
YOU AND I NOW KNOW.
HE DIDN'T KNOW THAT
FRIDAY'S TRAGEDY WOULD
BE SUNDAY'S TRIUMPH.

*No one yet knew from
the Scripture that he had
to rise from the dead.*

JOHN 20:9 MSG

March 13

THESE FINGERS FORMED ADAM OUT OF CLAY AND FURROWED TRUTH INTO TABLETS. WITH A WAVE, THIS HAND TOPPLED BABEL'S TOWER AND SPLIT THE RED SEA. FROM THIS HAND FLEW THE LOCUSTS THAT PLAGUED EGYPT AND THE RAVEN THAT FED ELIJAH. THE HAND OF GOD IS A MIGHTY HAND.

You drove out the nations with Your hand.... It was Your right hand, Your arm, and the light of Your countenance.

PSALM 44:2–3 NKJV

THREE YEARS EARLIER JOHN
HAD TURNED HIS BACK ON HIS
CAREER AND CAST HIS LOT
WITH THIS NAZARENE
CARPENTER. EARLIER IN THE
WEEK JOHN HAD ENJOYED A
TICKER-TAPE PARADE AS JESUS
AND THE DISCIPLES ENTERED
JERUSALEM. OH, HOW QUICKLY
THINGS HAD TURNED! THE
PEOPLE WHO HAD CALLED HIM
KING ON SUNDAY CALLED FOR
HIS DEATH THE FOLLOWING
FRIDAY. THESE LINENS WERE A
TANGIBLE REMINDER THAT HIS
FRIEND AND HIS FUTURE WERE
WRAPPED IN CLOTH AND
SEALED BEHIND A ROCK.

October 20

When they looked up, they saw
that the stone, which was very
large, had been rolled away.

MARK 16:4 NIV

OH, THE HANDS OF JESUS.
HANDS OF INCARNATION
AT HIS BIRTH. HANDS OF
LIBERATION AS HE HEALED.
HANDS OF INSPIRATION AS
HE TAUGHT. HANDS OF
DEDICATION AS HE SERVED.
AND HANDS OF
SALVATION AS HE DIED.

March 14

Look at my hands and my feet;
see that it is I myself.
Touch me and see.

LUKE 24:39 NRSV

JOHN COMMENTS ON THE
LINENS BECAUSE TO HIM
THEY WERE A PICTURE OF
FRIDAY'S TRAGEDY. AS
LONG AS THERE WERE NO
GRAVECLOTHES, AS LONG
AS THERE WAS NO TOMB,
AS LONG AS THERE WAS
NO CORONER, THERE
WAS HOPE. AND TO
THIS APOSTLE, THE
GRAVECLOTHES
SYMBOLIZED TRAGEDY.

October 19

*[Joseph and Nicodemus]
took Jesus' body and wrapped
it with the spices in pieces
of linen cloth, which is
how they bury the dead.*

JOHN 19:40 NCV

March 15

For God did not appoint us to suffer wrath but to receive salvation through our Lord Jesus Christ. He died for us so that, whether we are awake or asleep, we may live together with him. Therefore encourage one another and build each other up, just as in fact you are doing.

1 THESSALONIANS 5:9–11 NIV

October 18

Nicodemus brought seventy-five pounds of myrrh and aloes. The amount is worth noting, for such a quantity of burial ointments was typically used only for kings. God can turn any tragedy into a triumph, if only you will wait and watch.

Nicodemus, who earlier had come to Jesus at night, went with Joseph. He brought about seventy-five pounds of myrrh and aloes.

JOHN 19:39 NCV

BETWEEN JESUS' HAND AND
THE WOOD OF THE CROSS
THERE WAS A LIST. A LONG
LIST. A LIST OF OUR
MISTAKES. GOD HAS PENNED
A LIST OF OUR FAULTS.
THE LIST HE HAS MADE,
HOWEVER, CANNOT BE
READ. THE WORDS CAN'T
BE DECIPHERED. THE
MISTAKES ARE COVERED.
THE SINS ARE HIDDEN.
THOSE AT THE TOP ARE
HIDDEN BY HIS HAND; THOSE
DOWN THE LIST ARE
COVERED BY HIS BLOOD.
YOUR SINS ARE "BLOTTED
OUT" BY JESUS.

March 16

*But God commendeth his love
toward us, in that, while we were
yet sinners, Christ died for us.
Much more then, being now
justified by his blood, we shall be
saved from wrath through him.*

ROMANS 5:8–9 KJV

October 17

We all face tragedy. What's more, we've all received the symbols of tragedy. Yours might be a telegram from the war department, an ID bracelet from the hospital, a scar, or a court subpoena. We don't want these symbols. Like wrecked cars in a junkyard, they clutter up our hearts with memories of bad days. Could God use such things for something good?

In everything God works for the good of those who love him.

ROMANS 8:28 NCV

March 17

He died for all so that all who live—having received

eternal life from him—might live no longer for themselves,

to please themselves, but to spend their lives pleasing

Christ who died and rose again for them.

2 CORINTHIANS 5:15 TLB

October 16

For while we were still weak, at the right time Christ

died for the ungodly. Indeed, rarely will anyone die for a

righteous person—though perhaps for a good person

someone might actually dare to die. But God proves his

love for us in that while we still were sinners Christ died for us.

ROMANS 5:6–8 NRSV

THIS IS WHY JESUS REFUSED TO RESIST THE NAILS. HE SAW THE LIST OF YOUR MISTAKES BETWEEN HIS HAND AND THE WOOD OF THE CROSS! THIS WARRANT, THIS TABULATION OF YOUR FAILURES. HE KNEW THE PRICE OF THOSE SINS WAS DEATH. HE KNEW THE SOURCE OF THOSE SINS WAS YOU, AND SINCE HE COULDN'T BEAR THE THOUGHT OF ETERNITY WITHOUT YOU, HE CHOSE THE NAILS.

March 18

In love he predestined us to be adopted as his sons through Jesus Christ…to the praise of his glorious grace, which he has freely given us in the One he loves. In him we have redemption through his blood, the forgiveness of sins, in accordance with the riches of God's grace.

EPHESIANS 1:4–7 NIV

COULD GOD DO SOMETHING
SIMILAR IN YOUR LIFE?
COULD HE TAKE WHAT
TODAY IS A TOKEN OF
TRAGEDY AND TURN IT INTO
A SYMBOL OF TRIUMPH?
COULD SUCH A CHANGE
HAPPEN TO YOU? I HAVE
NO DOUBT. YOU SIMPLY
NEED TO DO WHAT JOHN
DID ON THAT SATURDAY
BEFORE THE RESURRECTION.
DON'T LEAVE. HANG OUT.

October 15

*I can do everything through
him who gives me strength.*

PHILIPPIANS 4:13 NIV

March 19

For Christ did not enter a sanctuary made by human hands,

a mere copy of the true one, but he entered into heaven itself,

now to appear in the presence of God on our behalf. Nor

was it to offer himself again and again, as the high priest

enters the Holy Place year after year with blood that is not his own;

for then he would have had to suffer again and again since the

foundation of the world. But as it is, he has appeared once for all at

the end of the age to remove sin by the sacrifice of himself.

HEBREWS 9:24–26 NRSV

THE APOSTLE JOHN CAME TO SEE BURIAL GARMENTS AS A SYMBOL OF TRIUMPH. HE DIDN'T ALWAYS SEE THEM THAT WAY. A TANGIBLE REMINDER OF THE DEATH OF HIS BEST FRIEND, THEY USED TO SEEM LIKE A SYMBOL OF TRAGEDY. BUT ON THE FIRST EASTER SUNDAY, GOD TOOK CLOTHING OF DEATH AND MADE IT A SYMBOL OF LIFE. COULD HE DO THE SAME FOR YOU?

October 14

I will be glad and rejoice in your love, for you saw my affliction and knew the anguish of my soul. You have not handed me over to the enemy but have set my feet in a spacious place.

PSALM 31:7–8 NIV

THE HAND SQUEEZING THE HANDLE OF THE MALLET WAS NOT A ROMAN INFANTRYMAN. THE FORCE BEHIND THE HAMMER WAS NOT AN ANGRY MOB. THE VERDICT BEHIND THE DEATH WAS NOT DECIDED BY JEALOUS JEWS. JESUS HIMSELF CHOSE THE NAILS.

March 20

In him we were also chosen, having been predestined according to the plan of him who works out everything in conformity with the purpose of his will.

EPHESIANS 1:11 NIV

GOD'S PROMISE
IN THE BURIAL
CLOTHING:
I CAN
TURN YOUR
TRAGEDY
INTO TRIUMPH.

October 13

*No, in all these things we are more than
conquerors through him who loved us. For I
am convinced that neither death nor life,
neither angels nor demons, neither the present
nor the future, nor any powers, neither height
nor depth, nor anything else in all creation,
will be able to separate us from the love of
God that is in Christ Jesus our Lord.*

ROMANS 8:37–39 NIV

JESUS WAS NO STRANGER TO THE DRIVING OF NAILS. AS A CARPENTER HE KNEW WHAT IT TOOK. AND AS A SAVIOR HE KNEW WHAT IT MEANT. HE KNEW THAT THE PURPOSE OF THE NAIL WAS TO PLACE YOUR SINS WHERE THEY COULD BE HIDDEN BY HIS SACRIFICE AND COVERED BY HIS BLOOD.

March 21

Blessed are they whose transgressions are forgiven, whose sins are covered. Blessed is the man whose sin the Lord will never count against him.

ROMANS 4:7, NIV

October 12

David, Paul, and Peter hit bottom, but they, like you, found their names on God's list of love. And you can be certain that the one who put it there knows how to pronounce it.

He who overcomes will, like them, be dressed in white. I will never blot out his name from the book of life, but will acknowledge his name before my Father and his angels.

REVELATION 3:5 NIV

March 22

Jesus was given to you, and…you put him to death by nailing him

to a cross. But this was God's plan which he had made long ago;

he knew all this would happen. God raised Jesus from the dead and

set him free from the pain of death, because death could not hold him.

Acts 2:23–24 NCV

October 11

God, who is rich in mercy, out of the great love with which he

loved us even when we were dead through our trespasses,

made us alive together with Christ—by grace you have been saved—

and raised us up with him and seated us with him in the heavenly

places in Christ Jesus.... For by grace you have been saved through

faith, and this is not your own doing; it is the gift of God.

EPHESIANS 2:4–8 NRSV

March 23

THE SAME HAND THAT STILLED THE SEAS STILLS YOUR GUILT. THE SAME HAND THAT CLEANSED THE TEMPLE CLEANSES YOUR HEART. THE HAND IS THE HAND OF GOD. THE NAIL IS THE NAIL OF GOD.

Because of the tender mercy of our God, by which the rising sun will come to us from heaven to shine on those living in darkness and in the shadow of death, to guide our feet into the path of peace.

LUKE 1:78-79 NIV

BUT ISN'T THERE A LIMIT?
SURELY THERE HAS TO BE
AN END TO THIS LOVE.
YOU'D THINK SO,
WOULDN'T YOU? BUT
DAVID THE ADULTERER
NEVER FOUND IT. PAUL
THE MURDERER NEVER
FOUND IT. PETER THE LIAR
NEVER FOUND IT. WHEN IT
CAME TO LIFE, THEY HIT
BOTTOM. BUT WHEN IT
CAME TO GOD'S LOVE,
THEY NEVER DID.

October 10

Your love, O Lord,
reaches to the heavens,
your faithfulness to the skies.

PSALM 36:5 NIV

March 24

GOD'S PROMISE
THROUGH THE SIGN:
I WILL SPEAK TO YOU
IN YOUR LANGUAGE.

*Pilate had a notice prepared
and fastened to the cross.
It read: JESUS OF NAZARETH,
THE KING OF THE JEWS....
And the sign was written in
Aramic, Latin and Greek.*

JOHN 19:19–20 NIV

IT'S NICE TO BE INCLUDED.
YOU AREN'T ALWAYS.
UNIVERSITIES EXCLUDE YOU
IF YOU AREN'T SMART
ENOUGH. BUSINESSES
EXCLUDE YOU IF YOU
AREN'T QUALIFIED ENOUGH,
AND, SADLY, SOME
CHURCHES EXCLUDE YOU IF
YOU AREN'T GOOD
ENOUGH. BUT THOUGH
THEY MAY EXCLUDE YOU,
CHRIST INCLUDES YOU.

October 9

But now in Christ Jesus
you who once were far away
have been brought near
through the blood of Christ.
EPHESIANS 2:13 NIV

March 25

I AM CERTAIN THAT WHEN
I ENTER THE PULPIT TO
PREACH OR STAND AT THE
LECTERN TO READ, IT IS
NOT MY WORD, BUT MY
TONGUE IS THE PEN OF A
READY WRITER.

MARTIN LUTHER

*So faith comes from what is
heard, and what is heard comes
through the word of Christ.*

ROMANS 10:17 NRSV

October 8

Because of his kindness you have been saved through trusting Christ.

And even trusting is not of yourselves; it too is a gift from God.

Salvation is not a reward for the good we have done, so none of us

can take any credit for it. It is God himself who has made us what we

are and given us new lives from Christ Jesus; and long ages ago he

planned that we should spend these lives in helping others.

EPHESIANS 2:8–10 TLB

THE FRAMER OF OUR
DESTINY IS FAMILIAR WITH
OUR DENSENESS. GOD
KNOWS WE SOMETIMES MISS
THE SIGNS. MAYBE THAT'S
WHY HE HAS GIVEN US SO
MANY. THE RAINBOW
AFTER THE FLOOD SIGNIFIES
GOD'S COVENANT.
CIRCUMCISION IDENTIFIES
GOD'S CHOSEN, AND THE
STARS PORTRAY THE SIZE
OF HIS FAMILY.

March 26

*I have set my rainbow in
the clouds, and it will be the
sign of the covenant between
me and the earth.*

GENESIS 9:13 NIV

WHEN ASKED TO DESCRIBE
THE WIDTH OF HIS LOVE,
JESUS STRETCHED ONE
HAND TO THE RIGHT AND
THE OTHER TO THE LEFT
AND HAD THEM NAILED IN
THAT POSITION SO YOU
WOULD KNOW HE DIED
LOVING YOU.

October 7

But the steadfast love of the
Lord is from everlasting to
everlasting on those who fear
him, and his righteousness to
children's children.

PSALM 103:17 NRSV

March 27

For what the law could not do, in that it was weak through the flesh, God sending his own Son in the likeness of sinful flesh, and for sin, condemned sin in the flesh: That the righteousness of the law might be fulfilled in us, who walk not after the flesh, but after the Spirit. For they that are after the flesh do mind the things of the flesh; but they that are after the Spirit the things of the Spirit.

ROMANS 8:3–5 KJV

October 6

Since we are surrounded by so great a cloud of witnesses,

let us also lay aside every weight and the sin that clings so closely,

and let us run with perseverance the race that is set before us, looking

to Jesus the pioneer and perfecter of our faith, who for the sake of the

joy that was set before him endured the cross, disregarding its shame,

and has taken his seat at the right hand of the throne of God.

Consider him who endured such hostility against himself from

sinners, so that you may not grow weary or lose heart.

HEBREWS 12:2–3 NRSV

March 28

Even today, we see signs in the New Testament church. Communion is a sign of His death, and baptism is a sign of our spiritual birth. Each of these signs symbolizes a greater spiritual truth.

Having been buried with him in baptism and raised with him through your faith in the power of God, who raised him from the dead.

Colossians 2:12 NIV

October 5

How wide is God's love?
Wide enough for the
whole world. Are you
included in the world?
Then you are included
in God's love.

*I have loved you with an
everlasting love; I have drawn
you with loving-kindness.*

Jeremiah 31:3 niv

WHY IS A SIGN PLACED OVER THE HEAD OF JESUS? WHY ARE THE WORDS WRITTEN IN THREE LANGUAGES, AND WHY IS THE SIGN MENTIONED IN ALL FOUR GOSPELS? OF ALL THE POSSIBLE ANSWERS TO THESE QUESTIONS, LET'S FOCUS ON ONE. COULD IT BE THAT THIS PIECE OF WOOD IS A PICTURE OF GOD'S DEVOTION? A SYMBOL OF HIS PASSION TO TELL THE WORLD ABOUT HIS SON? A REMINDER THAT GOD WILL DO WHATEVER IT TAKES TO SHARE WITH YOU THE MESSAGE OF THIS SIGN?

March 29

God's love was revealed among us in this way: God sent his only Son into the world so that we might live through him.

1 JOHN 4:9 NRSV

October 4

As boldly as the center beam of the cross proclaims God's holiness, the crossbeam declares his love. And, oh, how wide his love reaches.

For God so loved the world that he gave his one and only Son, that whoever believes in him shall not perish but have eternal life.

JOHN 3:16 NIV

I suggest that the sign on the cross reveals two truths about God's desire to reach the world. There is no person he will not use. There is no language he will not speak.

March 30

Pilate wrote a sign and put it on the cross. It read: JESUS OF NAZARETH, THE KING OF THE JEWS. *The sign was written in the Jewish language, in Latin, and in Greek.... What I have written, I have written.*

JOHN 19:19–20, 22 NCV

Consider what God did. He gave his Son. His only Son. Would you do that? Would you offer the life of your child for someone else? I wouldn't. There are those for whom I would give my life. But ask me to make a list of those for whom I would kill my daughter? The sheet will be blank. But God's list contains the name of every person who ever lived. For this is the scope of his love. And this is the reason for the cross. He loves the world.

October 3

This is how much God loved the world: He gave his Son, his one and only Son. And this is why: so that no one need be destroyed; by believing in him, anyone can have a whole and lasting life.

John 3:16 MSG

March 31

What an interesting choice of words. The thief on the cross doesn't plead, "Save me." He doesn't beg, "Have mercy on my soul." His appeal is that of a servant to a king.

Jesus, remember me when you come into your kingdom.

Luke 23:42 ncv

ENVISION THE MOMENT.
GOD ON HIS THRONE. YOU
ON THE EARTH. AND
BETWEEN YOU AND GOD,
SUSPENDED BETWEEN YOU
AND HEAVEN, IS CHRIST ON
HIS CROSS. YOUR SINS
HAVE BEEN PLACED ON
JESUS. GOD, WHO PUNISHES
SIN, RELEASES HIS RIGHTFUL
WRATH ON YOUR
MISTAKES. JESUS RECEIVES
THE BLOW. SINCE CHRIST IS
BETWEEN YOU AND GOD,
YOU DON'T. THE SIN IS
PUNISHED, BUT YOU ARE
SAFE—SAFE IN THE
SHADOW OF THE CROSS.

October 2

*We know the meaning of
those words because Jesus
Christ rescued us from this evil
world we're in by offering
himself as a sacrifice for our
sins. God's plan is that we
all experience that rescue.*

GALATIANS 1:4 MSG

April 1

For if, by the trespass of the one man, death reigned through that
one man, how much more will those who receive God's abundant
provision of grace and of the gift of righteousness reign in life
through the one man, Jesus Christ.

ROMANS 5:17 NIV

October 1

Christ carried our sins in his body on the cross so we would

stop living for sin and start living for what is right.... You were like

sheep that wandered away, but now you have come back

to the Shepherd and Protector of your souls.

1 PETER 2:24–25 NCV

THE THIEF ON THE CROSS
KNOWS HE IS IN A ROYAL
MESS. HE TURNS HIS HEAD
AND READS A ROYAL
PROCLAMATION AND
ASKS FOR ROYAL HELP. IT
MIGHT HAVE BEEN THIS
SIMPLE. IF SO, THE SIGN WAS
THE FIRST TOOL USED TO
PROCLAIM THE MESSAGE OF
THE CROSS.

April 2

The inscription of the charge against him read, "The King of the Jews." And with him they crucified two bandits, one on his right and one on his left.

MARK 15:26–27 NRSV

September 30

How could God forgive
our sins without
lowering his standards?

*Christ never sinned!
But God treated him as a
sinner, so that Christ could
make us acceptable to God.*

2 Corinthians 5:21 cev

COUNTLESS OTHER TOOLS HAVE BEEN USED TO PROCLAIM THE MESSAGE OF THE CROSS FROM THE PRINTING PRESS TO THE RADIO TO THE STADIUM CRUSADE. BUT A CRUDE WOODEN SIGN PRECEDED THEM ALL. AND BECAUSE OF THE SIGN, A SOUL WAS SAVED. ALL BECAUSE SOMEONE POSTED A SIGN ON A CROSS.

April 3

For the Jews require a sign, and the Greeks seek after wisdom: But we preach Christ crucified, unto the Jews a stumblingblock, and unto the Greeks foolishness; But unto them which are called…Christ the power of God, and the wisdom of God.

1 CORINTHIANS 1:22-24 NIV

September 29

THE HORIZONTAL BEAM OF
THE CROSS REPRESENTS THE
WIDTH OF GOD'S LOVE;
THE OTHER REFLECTS THE
HEIGHT OF HIS HOLINESS.
THE CROSS IS THE
INTERSECTION. THE CROSS
IS WHERE GOD FORGAVE
HIS CHILDREN WITHOUT
LOWERING HIS STANDARDS.
IN A SENTENCE: GOD PUT
OUR SIN ON HIS SON AND
PUNISHED IT THERE.

*He was pierced for our
transgressions, he was crushed
for our iniquities; the
punishment that brought us
peace was upon him, and by
his wounds we are healed.*

ISAIAH 53:5 NIV

April 4

The sign on the cross was Pilate's idea. God used a bush to call Moses and a donkey to convict a prophet. To get Jonah's attention, God used a big fish. There is no person he won't use.

If a man cleanses himself…
he will be an instrument for
noble purposes, made holy,
useful to the Master and
prepared to do any good work.

2 Timothy 2:21 NIV

September 28

WHY IS THE CROSS THE SYMBOL OF OUR FAITH? TO FIND THE ANSWER LOOK NO FARTHER THAN THE CROSS ITSELF. ITS DESIGN COULDN'T BE SIMPLER. ONE BEAM HORIZONTAL—THE OTHER VERTICAL. ONE REACHES OUT—LIKE GOD'S LOVE. THE OTHER REACHES UP— AS DOES GOD'S HOLINESS.

*For God was pleased…
through him to reconcile to
himself all things…by making
peace through his blood,
shed on the cross.*

COLOSSIANS 1:19–20 NIV

April 5

PILATE DID NOT INTEND TO SPREAD THE GOSPEL. IN FACT, THE SIGN ON THE CROSS SAID IN SO MANY WORDS, "THIS IS WHAT BECOMES OF A JEWISH KING; THIS IS WHAT THE ROMANS DO WITH HIM. THE KING OF THIS NATION IS A SLAVE; A CRUCIFIED CRIMINAL: AND IF SUCH BE THE KING, WHAT MUST THE NATION BE WHOSE KING HE IS?" PILATE HAD INTENDED THE SIGN TO THREATEN AND MOCK THE JEWS. BUT GOD HAD ANOTHER PURPOSE.

In his heart a man plans his course, but the Lord determines his steps.

PROVERBS 16:9 NIV

THE CROSS. CAN YOU
TURN ANY DIRECTION
WITHOUT SEEING ONE?
PERCHED ATOP A CHAPEL.
CARVED INTO A
GRAVEYARD HEADSTONE.
ENGRAVED IN A RING OR
SUSPENDED ON A CHAIN.
THE CROSS IS THE
UNIVERSAL SYMBOL OF
CHRISTIANITY. AN ODD
CHOICE, DON'T YOU THINK?
STRANGE THAT A TOOL
OF TORTURE WOULD COME
TO EMBODY A MOVEMENT
OF HOPE.

September 27

*We have put our hope
in the living God, who is
the Savior of all men.*

1 TIMOTHY 4:10 NIV

April 6

Where sin increased, grace increased all the more, so that,

just as sin reigned in death, so also grace might reign through

righteousness to bring eternal life through Jesus Christ our Lord.

ROMANS 5:20–21 NIV

September 26

Let us love one another, for love comes from God.

Everyone who loves has been born of God and knows God.

Whoever does not love does not know God, because God is love.

This is how God showed his love among us: He sent his one and

only Son into the world that we might live through him.

1 JOHN 4:7–9 NIV

April 7

Pilate was God's instrument for spreading the gospel. Unknown to himself, he was the amanuensis of heaven. He took dictation from God and wrote it on a sign. And the sign changed the destiny of a reader. There is no one God won't use.

But God chose the foolish things of the world to shame the wise; God chose the weak things of the world to shame the strong.

1 Corinthians 1:27 NIV

September 25

In the cross of Christ I glory,
Tow'ring o'er the wrecks of time;
All the light of sacred story
Gathers round its head sublime.

John Bowring

April 8

WE WOULDN'T LIKE TO IMAGINE THE TWENTIETH CENTURY WITHOUT C. S. LEWIS. IT WOULD BE HARD TO FIND A MORE PECULIAR EVANGELIST THAN THE ONE WHO LED LEWIS TO CHRIST. HIS NAME WAS T. D. WELDON. HE, LIKE C. S. LEWIS, WAS AGNOSTIC. BUT WELDON MADE A COMMENT ONE DAY THAT REROUTED LEWIS'S LIFE. HE HAD BEEN STUDYING A THEOLOGIAN'S DEFENSE OF THE GOSPELS. "RUM THING," HE COMMENTED, "THAT STUFF OF...THE DYING GOD. IT ALMOST LOOKS AS IF IT REALLY HAPPENED." THE STATEMENT...WAS ENOUGH TO CAUSE LEWIS TO CONSIDER THAT JESUS MIGHT ACTUALLY BE WHO HE CLAIMED TO BE.

September 24

Can a holy God overlook our mistakes? Can a kind God punish our mistakes? From our perspective there are only two equally unappealing solutions. But from his perspective there is a third. It's called "the Cross of Christ."

But God demonstrates his own love for us in this: While we were still sinners, Christ died for us.

Romans 5:8 NIV

April 9

A THIEF IS LED TO CHRIST BY ONE WHO REJECTED CHRIST. A SCHOLAR IS LED TO CHRIST BY ONE WHO DIDN'T BELIEVE IN CHRIST. THERE IS NO PERSON HE WILL NOT USE. AND, THERE IS NO LANGUAGE GOD WILL NOT SPEAK.

Though I have been speaking figuratively, a time is coming when I will no longer use this kind of language but will tell you plainly about my Father.

JOHN 16:25 NIV

September 23

GOD'S PROMISE
IN THE CROSS:
I WILL LOVE
YOU FOREVER.

Because of his great love for us, God,

who is rich in mercy, made us alive

with Christ even when we were dead

in transgressions…that in the coming

ages he might show the incomparable

riches of his grace, expressed in his

kindness to us in Christ Jesus.

EPHESIANS 2:4–5,7 NIV

EVERY PASSERBY COULD
READ HEBREW, LATIN, OR
GREEK—THE THREE GREAT
LANGUAGES OF THE
ANCIENT WORLD.
"HEBREW WAS THE
LANGUAGE OF ISRAEL,
THE LANGUAGE OF
RELIGION; LATIN THE
LANGUAGE OF THE
ROMANS, THE LANGUAGE
OF LAW AND
GOVERNMENT; AND GREEK
THE LANGUAGE OF
GREECE, THE LANGUAGE
OF CULTURE. CHRIST
WAS DECLARED KING
IN THEM ALL."

April 10

Above his head they placed the

written charge against him:

THIS IS JESUS, THE

KING OF THE JEWS.

MATTHEW 27:37 NIV

WHEN YOU AND I STAND IN HEAVEN TO RECEIVE OUR PRIZE, ONLY ONE WILL KNOW ALL OF OUR SINS, BUT HE WON'T EMBARRASS YOU—HE HAS ALREADY FORGIVEN THEM. SO ENJOY THE GAME, MY FRIEND; YOUR PRIZE IS SECURE. BUT YOU MIGHT ASK THE TEACHER FOR SOME HELP WITH THAT SWING.

September 22

If we confess our sins, he is faithful and just to forgive us our sins, and to cleanse us from all unrighteousness.

1 JOHN 1:9 KJV

April 11

How much more, then, will the blood of Christ, who through the eternal Spirit offered himself unblemished to God, cleanse our consciences from acts that lead to death, so that we may serve the living God! For this reason Christ is the mediator of a new covenant, that those who are called may receive the promised eternal inheritance—now that he has died as a ransom to set them free from the sins committed under the first covenant.

HEBREWS 9:14–15 NIV

September 21

As God's chosen ones, holy and beloved, clothe yourselves with
compassion, kindness, humility, meekness, and patience.
Bear with one another and, if anyone has a complaint against
another, forgive each other; just as the Lord has forgiven you,
so you also must forgive. Above all, clothe yourselves with love,
which binds everything together in perfect harmony.

COLOSSIANS 3:12–14 NRSV

EVERY PASSERBY COULD READ THE SIGN. GOD HAD A MESSAGE FOR EACH. "CHRIST IS KING." THE MESSAGE WAS THE SAME, BUT THE LANGUAGES WERE DIFFERENT. SINCE JESUS WAS A KING FOR ALL PEOPLE, THE MESSAGE WOULD BE IN THE TONGUES OF ALL PEOPLE.

April 12

I truly understand that God shows no partiality, but in every nation anyone who fears him and does what is right is acceptable to him. You know the message he sent to the people of Israel, preaching peace by Jesus Christ—he is Lord of all.

ACTS 10:34–36 NRSV

JESUS ALLOWS YOUR
MISTAKES TO BE LOST IN HIS
PERFECTION. AS THE FOUR
OF US GOLFERS STOOD IN
THE CLUBHOUSE TO RECEIVE
THE AWARD, THE ONLY
ONES WHO KNEW OF THE
POVERTY OF MY GAME
WERE MY TEAMMATES,
AND THEY DIDN'T TELL.

September 20

Blessed are they whose

transgressions are forgiven,

whose sins are covered.

ROMANS 4:7 NIV

April 13

There is no language God will not speak. Which leads us to a delightful question. What language is he speaking to you? I'm not referring to an idiom or dialect but to the day-to-day drama of your life. God does speak, you know. He speaks to us in whatever language we will understand.

Speak, Lord, for your servant is listening.
1 Samuel 3:9 NRSV

ENGRAVE IN YOUR HEART
THE ANNOUNCEMENT OF
JOHN THE BAPTIST. JESUS IS
"THE LAMB OF GOD, WHO
TAKES AWAY THE SIN OF
THE WORLD" (JOHN 1:29).
THE BLOOD OF CHRIST
DOES NOT COVER YOUR
SINS, CONCEAL YOUR SINS,
POSTPONE YOUR SINS, OR
DIMINISH YOUR SINS. IT
TAKES AWAY YOUR SINS,
ONCE AND FOR ALL TIME.

September 19

And the blood of Jesus Christ

His Son cleanses us from all sin.

1 JOHN 1:7 NKJV

April 14

There are times God speaks the "language of abundance." Is your tummy full? Are your bills paid? Got a little jingle in your pocket? Don't be so proud of what you have that you miss what you need to hear. Could it be you have much so you can give much?

God can give you more blessings than you need. Then you will always have plenty of everything—enough to give to every good work.

2 Corinthians 9:8 ncv

PERHAPS YOU ALWAYS
SERVE FOR FEAR OF NOT
BEING SAVED. PERHAPS YOU
DON'T TRUST YOUR TEAM.
YOU'RE WORRIED THAT A
SECRET CARD EXISTS ON
WHICH YOUR SCORE IS
BEING WRITTEN. IS THAT
YOU? IF SO, KNOW THIS:
THE BLOOD OF JESUS IS
ENOUGH TO SAVE YOU.

September 18

*For you know that it was not
with perishable things such as
silver or gold that you were
redeemed…but with the
precious blood of Christ, a lamb
without blemish or defect.*

1 PETER 1:18–19 NIV

April 15

IS GOD TALKING IN THE "LANGUAGE OF ABUNDANCE"? OR ARE YOU HEARING THE "VERNACULAR OF WANT"? WE'D RATHER HE SPOKE THE LANGUAGE OF ABUNDANCE, BUT HE DOESN'T ALWAYS.

I know what it is to be in need, and I know what it is to have plenty. I have learned the secret of being content in any and every situation, whether well fed or hungry, whether living in plenty or in want.

PHILIPPIANS 4:12 NIV

September 17

Do you feel so saved that you never serve? Are you so happy with the score of your team that you aren't getting out of the golf cart? If that is you, let me ask a question. Why does God have you on the course? Why didn't he beam you up the moment he saved you? The fact is, you and I are here for a reason, and that reason is to glorify God in our service.

So whether you eat or drink or whatever you do, do it all for the glory of God.

1 Corinthians 10:31 niv

April 16

Rejoice in the Lord your God, for he has given you the autumn rains in righteousness. He sends you abundant showers, both autumn and spring rains....You will have plenty to eat, until you are full, and you will praise the name of the Lord your God, who has worked wonders for you.

JOEL 2:23,26 NIV

September 16

Because of his kindness you have been saved through trusting Christ.

And even trusting is not of yourselves; it too is a gift from God.

Salvation is not a reward for the good we have done, so none of us

can take any credit for it. It is God himself who has made us what

we are and given us new lives from Christ Jesus; and long ages ago

he planned that we should spend these lives in helping others.

<small>EPHESIANS 2:8–10 TLB</small>

THE BIRTH OF OUR FIRST CHILD
COINCIDED WITH THE CANCELLATION
OF OUR HEALTH INSURANCE.
DENALYN AND I WERE LEFT WITH THE
JOY OF AN EIGHT-POUND BABY GIRL
AND THE BURDEN OF A TWENTY-FIVE-
HUNDRED-DOLLAR HOSPITAL BILL.
A FEW WEEKS LATER I SPOKE AT
A RETREAT FOR A SMALL CHURCH
IN FLORIDA. A MEMBER OF THE
CONGREGATION HANDED ME AN
ENVELOPE AND SAID, "THIS IS FOR
YOUR FAMILY." I EXPECTED THE
AMOUNT TO BE FIFTY OR A HUNDRED
DOLLARS. BUT WHEN I OPENED THE
ENVELOPE, THE CHECK WAS FOR
TWENTY-FIVE HUNDRED DOLLARS.
THROUGH THE LANGUAGE OF NEED,
GOD SPOKE TO ME.

April 17

*But if God so clothes
the grass of the field…will he
not much more clothe you—
you of little faith?*

MATTHEW 6:30 NRSV

"At once blood and water came out" (John 19:34). John doesn't emphasize one over the other. But, oh, how we do. Some accept the blood but forget the water. They want to be saved but don't want to be changed. Others accept the water but forget the blood. They are busy for Christ but never at peace in Christ. The blood is God's sacrifice for us. The water is God's Spirit in us. And we need both.

September 15

God presented him as a sacrifice of atonement, through faith in his blood. He did this to demonstrate his justice, because in his forbearance he had left the sins committed beforehand unpunished.

ROMANS 3:25 NIV

April 18

THROUGH THE LANGUAGE
OF NEED, GOD SPEAKS TO
US. IT IS AS IF HE SAYS, "I'M
INVOLVED IN YOUR LIFE. I
WILL TAKE CARE OF YOU."

_My God will meet all your
needs according to his glorious
riches in Christ Jesus._

PHILIPPIANS 4:19 NIV

September 14

CAN YOU BE MORE SAVED
THAN YOU WERE THE FIRST
DAY OF YOUR SALVATION?
NO. BUT CAN A PERSON
GROW IN SALVATION?
ABSOLUTELY. IT, LIKE
MARRIAGE, IS A DONE
DEAL AND A DAILY
DEVELOPMENT.

*Now he has reconciled you
by Christ's physical body
through death to present you
holy in his sight, without
blemish and free from
accusation—if you continue in
your faith, established and firm.*

COLOSSIANS 1:22–23 NIV

ARE YOU HEARING THE
"LANGUAGE OF NEED"?
OR HOW ABOUT THE
"LANGUAGE OF AFFLICTION"?
TALK ABOUT AN IDIOM WE
AVOID. BUT YOU AND I BOTH
KNOW HOW CLEARLY GOD
SPEAKS IN HOSPITAL
HALLWAYS AND SICKBEDS.
WE KNOW WHAT DAVID
MEANT WITH THE WORDS,
"HE MAKES ME TO LIE DOWN"
(PS. 23:2). NOTHING SEEMS
TO TURN OUR EARS TOWARD
HEAVEN LIKE A FRAIL BODY.

April 19

Trust in the Lord forever,

for in the Lord God you

have an everlasting rock.

ISAIAH 26:4 NRSV

TECHNICALLY, ON THEIR FIFTIETH ANNIVERSARY A BRIDE AND GROOM ARE NO MORE UNITED THAN THEY WERE WHEN THEY LEFT THE ALTAR. BUT RELATIONALLY, THEY ARE COMPLETELY DIFFERENT. MARRIAGE IS BOTH A DONE DEAL AND A DAILY DEVELOPMENT, SOMETHING YOU DID AND SOMETHING YOU DO. THE SAME IS TRUE OF OUR WALK WITH GOD.

September 13

Let us rejoice and exult and give him the glory, for the marriage of the Lamb has come, and his bride has made herself ready.

REVELATION 19:7 NRSV

April 20

GOD SPEAKS ALL
LANGUAGES—INCLUDING
YOURS. HAS HE NOT SAID,
"I WILL...TEACH YOU IN THE
WAY YOU SHOULD GO"
(Ps. 32:8)? ARE WE NOT
URGED TO "RECEIVE
INSTRUCTION FROM HIS
MOUTH" (JOB 22:22)?
WHAT LANGUAGE IS GOD
SPEAKING TO YOU?

I will instruct you and teach
you in the way you should go;
I will counsel you and
watch over you.

PSALM 32:8 NIV

ARE A BRIDE AND GROOM
EVER MORE MARRIED THAN
THEY ARE THE FIRST DAY?
THE VOWS ARE MADE AND
THE CERTIFICATE SIGNED—
COULD THEY BE ANY MORE
MARRIED THAN THAT?
PERHAPS THEY COULD.
WOULDN'T THEY HAVE TO BE
MORE MARRIED ON THEIR
FIFTIETH ANNIVERSARY THAN
ON THEIR WEDDING DAY?
YET, ON THE OTHER HAND,
HOW COULD THEY BE? THE
MARRIAGE CERTIFICATE
HASN'T MATURED. AH, BUT
THE RELATIONSHIP HAS, AND
THERE IS THE DIFFERENCE.

September 12

But speaking the truth in love,
we must grow up in every
way into him who is the head,
into Christ.

EPHESIANS 4:15 NRSV

April 21

I am the Vine, you are the branches. When you're joined with me and I with you, the relation intimate and organic, the harvest is sure to be abundant. Separated, you can't produce a thing.... But if you make yourselves at home with me and my words are at home in you, you can be sure that whatever you ask will be listened to and acted upon.

JOHN 15:5-7 MSG

September 11

He saved us, not because of any works of righteousness that we had done, but according to his mercy, through the water of rebirth and renewal by the Holy Spirit. This Spirit he poured out on us richly through Jesus Christ our Savior, so that, having been justified by his grace, we might become heirs according to the hope of eternal life.

TITUS 3:5–7 NRSV

April 22

Aren't you glad he is speaking? Aren't you grateful that he cares enough to talk? Isn't it good to know that "the Lord tells his secrets to those who respect him" (Ps. 25:14)?

The Lord confides in those who fear him; he makes his covenant known to them.

PSALM 25:14 NIV

As a result of "being saved" (the work of the blood), what do we do? We obey God "with deep reverence" and shrink back "from all that might displease him." Do we do this in order to be saved? No. These are "the good things that result from being saved."

Do the good things that result from being saved, obeying God with deep reverence, shrinking back from all that might displease him. For God is at work within you, helping you want to obey him, and then helping you do what he wants.

PHILIPIANS 2:12–13 TLB

April 23

YOUR FATHER HAS
LEARNED TO SPEAK
YOUR LANGUAGE.

It has been given to you to
know the mysteries of the
kingdom of heaven.

MATTHEW 13:11 NKJV

September 9

WATER IS A PICTURE OF
THE SPIRIT OF JESUS
WORKING IN US. HE'S NOT
WORKING TO SAVE US,
MIND YOU; THAT WORK
IS DONE. HE'S WORKING
TO CHANGE US.

*I will sprinkle clean water
on you, and you will be clean;
I will cleanse you from
all your impurities.*

EZEKIEL 36:25 NIV

ASK GOD IF YOU MIGHT BE
MISSING ANY SIGNS HE IS
SENDING YOUR WAY. IT'S
ONE THING TO MISS A
MESSAGE FROM YOUR WIFE
ABOUT CLEANING UP A
ROOM. IT'S SOMETHING ELSE
ENTIRELY TO MISS ONE
FROM GOD ABOUT THE
DESTINY OF YOUR LIFE.

April 24

*How great are his signs, how
mighty his wonders! His
kingdom is an everlasting
kingdom, and his sovereignty is
from generation to generation.*

DANIEL 4:3 NRSV

September 8

"If anyone believes in me, rivers of living water will flow out from that person's heart, as the Scripture says." Jesus was talking about the Holy Spirit. The Spirit had not yet been given, because Jesus had not yet been raised to glory. But later, those who believed in Jesus would receive the Spirit.

JOHN 7:38–39 NCV

April 25

GOD'S PROMISE THROUGH
THE TWO CROSSES:
I WILL LET
YOU CHOOSE.

*One of the criminals on a cross
began to shout insults at
Jesus…. But the other criminal
stopped him and said, "You
should fear God!…" Then he
said, "Jesus, remember me when
you come into your kingdom."*

LUKE 23:39–40,42 NCV

REMEMBER THE WORDS OF
JESUS TO THE SAMARITAN
WOMAN? "THE WATER I
GIVE WILL BECOME A
SPRING OF WATER GUSHING
UP INSIDE THAT PERSON,
GIVING ETERNAL LIFE"
(JOHN 4:14). JESUS OFFERS,
NOT A SINGULAR DRINK OF
WATER, BUT A PERPETUAL
ARTESIAN WELL! AND THE
WELL ISN'T A HOLE IN
YOUR BACKYARD BUT
THE HOLY SPIRIT OF
GOD IN YOUR HEART.

September 7

*Let the one who believes in
me drink. As the scripture
has said, "Out of the
believer's heart shall flow
rivers of living water."*

JOHN 7:38 NRSV

April 26

Strive to enter through the narrow door; for many, I tell you, will try to enter and will not be able. When once the owner of the house has got up and shut the door, and you begin to stand outside and to knock at the door, saying, 'Lord, open to us,' then in reply he will say to you, 'I do not know where you come from.'

LUKE 13:24-25 NRSV

September 6

You have died to the law through the body of Christ, so that you

may belong to another, to him who has been raised from the dead in

order that we may bear fruit for God. While we were living in the

flesh, our sinful passions, aroused by the law, were at work in our

members to bear fruit for death. But now we are discharged from the

law, dead to that which held us captive, so that we are slaves not

under the old written code but in the new life of the Spirit.

ROMANS 7:4–6 NRSV

ABEL AND CAIN, BOTH SONS OF ADAM. ABEL CHOOSES GOD. CAIN CHOOSES MURDER. AND GOD LETS HIM. ABRAHAM AND LOT, BOTH PILGRIMS IN CANAAN. ABRAHAM CHOOSES GOD. LOT CHOOSES SODOM. AND GOD LETS HIM. DAVID AND SAUL, BOTH KINGS OF ISRAEL. DAVID CHOOSES GOD. SAUL CHOOSES POWER. AND GOD LETS HIM. PETER AND JUDAS, BOTH DENY THEIR LORD. PETER SEEKS MERCY. JUDAS SEEKS DEATH. AND GOD LETS HIM. IN EVERY AGE OF HISTORY, ON EVERY PAGE OF SCRIPTURE, THE TRUTH IS REVEALED: GOD ALLOWS US TO MAKE OUR OWN CHOICES.

April 27

Immediately the rooster crowed the second time. Then Peter remembered the word Jesus had spoken to him: "Before the rooster crows twice you will disown me three times."

MARK 14:72 NIV

September 5

IF THE SACRIFICE HAS BEEN
OFFERED ONCE AND FOR
ALL TIME, NEED IT BE
OFFERED AGAIN? OF
COURSE NOT. THE WORK
FOR US IS COMPLETE, BUT
THE PROGRESSIVE WORK IN
US IS ONGOING. IF HIS WORK
FOR US IS SEEN IN THE
BLOOD, WHAT MIGHT THE
WATER REPRESENT? YOU
GOT IT. HIS WORK IN US.

*He saved us, not because
of righteous things we had
done, but because of his mercy.
He saved us through the
washing of rebirth and
renewal by the Holy Spirit.*

TITUS 3:5 NIV

April 28

GOD ALLOWS US TO MAKE
OUR OWN CHOICES. AND
NO ONE DELINEATES THIS
MORE CLEARLY THAN JESUS.
ACCORDING TO HIM, WE
CAN CHOOSE: A NARROW
GATE OR A WIDE GATE, A
NARROW ROAD OR A WIDE
ROAD, THE BIG CROWD OR
THE SMALL CROWD.

*Enter through the narrow gate.
For wide is the gate and broad
is the road that leads to
destruction, and many enter
through it. But small is the gate
and narrow the road that leads
to life, and only a few find it.*

MATTHEW 7:13–14 NIV

September 4

WHAT NEEDED TO BE PAID WAS PAID. WHAT HAD TO BE DONE WAS DONE. INNOCENT BLOOD WAS REQUIRED. INNOCENT BLOOD WAS OFFERED, ONCE AND FOR ALL TIME. BURY THOSE FIVE WORDS DEEP IN YOUR HEART. ONCE AND FOR ALL TIME.

When [Christ] had offered for all time one sacrifice for sins, he sat down at the right hand of God…because by one sacrifice he has made perfect forever those who are being made holy.

HEBREWS 10:12,14 NIV

ON THE WOOD OF THE
CROSS THE WORLD WAS
SAVED ALL AT ONCE, AND
WHOEVER IS LOST LOSES
HIMSELF, BECAUSE HE WILL
NOT RECEIVE THE SAVIOUR,
BECAUSE HE FALLS AGAIN
AND REPEATS THE FALL
OF ADAM.

COUNT NIKOLAUS LUDWIG
VON ZINZENDORF

April 29

*For the message about the
cross is foolishness to those
who are perishing, but to
us who are being saved it
is the power of God.*

1 CORINTHIANS 1:18 NRSV

September 3

THE SON OF GOD BECAME THE LAMB OF GOD, THE CROSS BECAME THE ALTAR.

For you know that it was not with perishable things such as silver or gold that you were redeemed from the empty way of life handed down to you from your forefathers, but with the precious blood of Christ, a lamb without blemish or defect.

1 PETER 1:18-19 NIV

April 30

GOD ALLOWS US TO MAKE OUR OWN CHOICES. AND NO ONE DELINEATES THIS MORE CLEARLY THAN JESUS. ACCORDING TO HIM, WE CAN CHOOSE TO: BUILD ON ROCK OR SAND, SERVE GOD OR RICHES, OR BE NUMBERED AMONG THE SHEEP OR THE GOATS.

No one can serve two masters....You cannot serve both God and Money.

MATTHEW 6:24 NIV

September 2

AFTER CHRIST'S SACRIFICE
THERE WOULD BE NO MORE
NEED TO SHED BLOOD.

*Once for all [Christ] took blood
into that inner room, the Holy
of Holies, and sprinkled it on
the mercy seat; but it was not
the blood of goats and calves.
No, he took his own blood, and
with it he, by himself, made
sure of our eternal salvation.*

HEBREWS 9:12 TLB

May 1

I tell you the truth, whoever hears my word and believes him

who sent me has eternal life and will not be condemned;

he has crossed over from death to life. I tell you the truth, a time is

coming and has now come when the dead will hear the voice of the

Son of God and those who hear will live. For as the Father has

life in himself, so he has granted the Son to have life in himself.

JOHN 5:24-26 NIV

September 1

Lead me in your truth, and teach me, for you are the God of my salvation; for you I wait all day long. Be mindful of your mercy, O Lord, and of your steadfast love, for they have been from of old. Do not remember the sins of my youth or my transgressions; according to your steadfast love remember me, for your goodness' sake.

PSALM 25:5-7 NRSV

May 2

GOD GIVES ETERNAL
CHOICES, AND THESE
CHOICES HAVE ETERNAL
CONSEQUENCES.

*Then they [those who
rejected God] will go away
to eternal punishment,
but the righteous to eternal life.*

MATTHEW 25:46 NIV

WHAT ABEL SOUGHT TO
ACCOMPLISH IN THE FIELD,
GOD ACHIEVED WITH HIS
SON. WHAT ABEL BEGAN,
CHRIST COMPLETED. AFTER
HIS SACRIFICE THERE
WOULD BE NO MORE
SACRIFICIAL SYSTEM.

August 31

*He came as High Priest
of this better system which
we now have.*

HEBREWS 9:11 TLB

May 3

Ever wonder why there were two crosses next to Christ? Why not six or ten? Ever wonder why Jesus was in the center? Why not on the far right or far left? Could it be that the two crosses on the hill symbolize one of God's greatest gifts? The gift of choice.

There Jesus was nailed to the cross, and on each side of him a man was also nailed to a cross.

JOHN 19:18 CEV

THOSE WHO OFFERED A
BLOOD SACRIFICE FOR SINS
FORM A LONG LINE:
ABRAHAM, MOSES, GIDEON,
SAMSON, SAUL, DAVID....
THEY KNEW THE SHEDDING OF
BLOOD WAS NECESSARY FOR
THE FORGIVENESS OF SINS.
JACOB KNEW IT TOO; HENCE,
THE STONES WERE STACKED
FOR THE ALTAR. SOLOMON
KNEW IT, AND THE TEMPLE
WAS BUILT. AARON KNEW IT;
THEREFORE, THE PRIESTHOOD
BEGAN. HAGGAI AND
ZECHARIAH KNEW IT; AS A
RESULT, THE TEMPLE WAS
BUILT AGAIN.

August 30

*And almost all things are by
the law purged with blood.*

HEBREWS 9:22 KJV

THE TWO CRIMINALS CRUCIFIED WITH JESUS HAVE SO MUCH IN COMMON. CONVICTED BY THE SAME SYSTEM. CONDEMNED TO THE SAME DEATH. BUT ONE CHANGED. WHILE WE REJOICE AT THE THIEF WHO CHANGED, DARE WE FORGET THE ONE WHO DIDN'T? WHAT ABOUT HIM, JESUS? WOULDN'T A PERSONAL INVITATION BE APPROPRIATE? WOULDN'T A WORD OF PERSUASION BE TIMELY? JESUS GAVE HIM THE CHOICE. HE GAVE BOTH CRIMINALS THE SAME.

May 4

One of the criminals who were hanged there kept deriding him and saying, "Are you not the Messiah? Save yourself and us!" But the other rebuked him, saying, "Do you not fear God, since you are under the same sentence of condemnation?"

LUKE 23:39–40 NRSV

August 29

How Abel knew that is anyone's guess, but somehow he knew to offer more than prayers and crops. He knew to offer a life. He knew to pour out more than his heart and his desires; he knew to pour out blood.

Abel for his part brought of the firstlings of his flock....
And the Lord had regard for Abel and his offering.

GENESIS 4:4 NRSV

May 5

THERE ARE TIMES
WHEN GOD SENDS
THUNDER TO STIR US.
THERE ARE TIMES
WHEN GOD SENDS
BLESSINGS TO LURE US.
BUT THEN THERE ARE
TIMES WHEN GOD
SENDS NOTHING BUT
SILENCE AS HE HONORS
US WITH THE FREEDOM
TO CHOOSE WHERE WE
SPEND ETERNITY.

*"Go out, and stand on the mountain before
the Lord." And behold, the Lord passed by,
and a great and strong wind tore into the
mountains and broke the rocks in pieces
before the Lord, but the Lord was not
in the wind; and after the wind an
earthquake, but the Lord was not in the
earthquake; and after the earthquake a fire,
but the Lord was not in the fire.*

1 KINGS 19:11-12 NKJV

August 28

[Jesus] entered once for all into the Holy Place, not with the blood of goats and calves, but with his own blood, thus obtaining eternal redemption. For if the blood of goats and bulls, with the sprinkling of the ashes of a heifer, sanctifies those who have been defiled so that their flesh is purified, how much more will the blood of Christ, who through the eternal Spirit offered himself without blemish to God, purify our conscience from dead works to worship the living God!

HEBREWS 9:12–14 NRSV

May 6

Be all the more eager to make your calling and election sure.

For if you do these things, you will never fall,

and you will receive a rich welcome into the eternal

kingdom of our Lord and Savior Jesus Christ.

2 PETER 1:10-11 NIV

August 27

"BUT ONE OF THE SOLDIERS STUCK HIS SPEAR INTO JESUS' SIDE, AND AT ONCE BLOOD AND WATER CAME OUT" (JOHN 19:34). EVEN A CASUAL STUDENT OF SCRIPTURE NOTES THE CONNECTION BETWEEN BLOOD AND MERCY.

Without the shedding of blood there is no forgiveness.

HEBREWS. 9:22 NIV

IN SO MANY AREAS OF LIFE
WE HAVE NO CHOICE.
THINK ABOUT IT. YOU
DIDN'T CHOOSE YOUR
GENDER. YOU DIDN'T
CHOOSE YOUR SIBLINGS.
YOU DIDN'T CHOOSE YOUR
RACE OR PLACE OF BIRTH.
SOMETIMES OUR LACK OF
CHOICES ANGERS US.
BUT GOD HONORS US
WITH THE FREEDOM TO
CHOOSE WHERE WE
SPEND ETERNITY.

May 7

I have set before you life and death.... Now choose life.

DEUTERONOMY 30:19 NIV

POSITIONAL AND PROGRESSIVE SANCTIFICATION. GOD'S WORK FOR US AND GOD'S WORK IN US. NEGLECT THE FIRST, AND YOU GROW FEARFUL. NEGLECT THE SECOND, AND YOU GROW LAZY. BOTH ARE ESSENTIAL, AND BOTH ARE SEEN IN THE MOISTENED DIRT AT THE BASE OF THE CROSS OF CHRIST.

August 26

So we are ambassadors for Christ, since God is making his appeal through us; we entreat you on behalf of Christ, be reconciled to God.

2 CORINTHIANS 5:20 NRSV

THE SCALES OF LIFE WERE
FOREVER TIPPED ON THE
SIDE OF FAIRNESS WHEN
GOD PLANTED A TREE IN
THE GARDEN OF EDEN. ALL
COMPLAINTS WERE
SILENCED WHEN ADAM
AND HIS DESCENDANTS
WERE GIVEN FREE WILL,
THE FREEDOM TO MAKE
WHATEVER ETERNAL
CHOICE WE DESIRE. ANY
INJUSTICE IN THIS LIFE IS
OFFSET BY THE HONOR OF
CHOOSING OUR DESTINY
IN THE NEXT.

May 8

And the Lord God planted a
garden in Eden…. Out of the
ground the Lord God
made…the tree of the
knowledge of good and evil.

GENESIS 2:8–9 NRSV

August 25

It was necessary, then, for the copies of the heavenly things to be purified with these sacrifices, but the heavenly things themselves with better sacrifices than these. For Christ did not enter a man-made sanctuary that was only a copy of the true one; he entered heaven itself, now to appear for us in God's presence. Nor did he enter heaven to offer himself again and again, the way the high priest enters the Most Holy Place every year with blood that is not his own.

HEBREWS 9:23–25 NIV

May 9

For this one man, Adam, brought death to many through his sin.
But this one man, Jesus Christ, brought forgiveness to many through
God's mercy. *Adam's* one *sin brought the penalty of death to*
many, while Christ freely takes away many *sins and gives glorious*
life instead. The *sin of this one man, Adam, caused* death to be
king over all, *but all who will take God's gift of forgiveness and*
acquittal are kings of life because of this one man, Jesus Christ.

ROMANS 5:15–17 TLB

Positional sanctification comes because of Christ's work for us. Progressive sanctification comes because of Christ's work in us. Both are gifts from God. "With one sacrifice he made perfect forever those who are being made holy" (Heb. 10:14). See the blending of tenses? "He made perfect" (positional sanctification) those who are "being made holy" (progressive sanctification).

August 24

But when Christ had offered for all time a single sacrifice for sins, "he sat down at the right hand of God," and since then has been waiting "until his enemies would be made a footstool for his feet." For by a single offering he has perfected for all time those who are sanctified.

Hebrews 10:12–14 NRSV

Would you have preferred that you choose everything in this life, and God chooses where you spend the next? You choose the size of your nose, the color of your hair, and your DNA structure, and he chooses where you spend eternity? God honors us with the freedom to choose where we spend eternity.

May 10

For God so loved the world,
that he gave his only begotten
Son, that whosoever believeth
in him should not perish,
but have everlasting life.

John 3:16 KJV

August 23

But God is so rich in mercy; he loved us so much that even though we were spiritually dead and doomed by our sins, he gave us back our lives again when he raised Christ from the dead—only by his undeserved favor have we ever been saved—and lifted us up from the grave into glory along with Christ, where we sit with him in the heavenly realms—all because of what Christ Jesus did.

EPHESIANS 2:5–7 TLB

May 11

He has rescued us from the power of darkness and transferred us

into the kingdom of his beloved Son, in whom we have

redemption, the forgiveness of sins. He is the image of the

invisible God, the firstborn of all creation; for in him all things

in heaven and on earth were created, things visible and invisible,

whether thrones or dominions or rulers or powers—

all things have been created through him and for him.

COLOSSIANS 1:13–16 NRSV

A SECOND TERM WAS
ILLUSTRATED IN THAT GOLF
GAME: "PROGRESSIVE
SANCTIFICATION." THOUGH I
OFFERED SO LITTLE IN THE
PRO-AM TOURNAMENT, I
IMPROVED WITH EACH HOLE. MY
FRIEND BUDDY KEPT GIVING ME
TIPS AND CHANGING MY GRIP
UNTIL FINALLY I MADE A
CONTRIBUTION. I IMPROVED
PROGRESSIVELY. THE PRIZE CAME
BECAUSE OF BUDDY'S SCORE. THE
IMPROVEMENT CAME BECAUSE OF
BUDDY'S HELP. POSITIONAL
SANCTIFICATION COMES BECAUSE
OF CHRIST'S WORK FOR US.
PROGRESSIVE SANCTIFICATION
COMES BECAUSE OF CHRIST'S
WORK IN US.

August 22

May the God of peace…
equip you with everything
good for doing his will, and
may he work in us what is
pleasing to him, through Jesus
Christ, to whom be glory
for ever and ever. Amen.

HEBREWS 13:20–21 NIV

It would have been nice if God had let us order life like we order a meal. I'll take good health and a high IQ. I'll pass on the music skills, but give me a fast metabolism.... Would've been nice. But it didn't happen. When it came to your life on earth, you weren't given a voice or a vote. But when it comes to life after death, you were. In my book that seems like a good deal.

May 12

Now we have received not the spirit of the world, but the Spirit that is from God, so that we may understand the gifts bestowed on us by God.

1 Corinthians 2:12 NRSV

August 21

THE TWO-DOLLAR
THEOLOGICAL TERM
FOR THIS IS POSITIONAL
SANCTIFICATION. SIMPLY
DEFINED: YOU ARE GIVEN
A PRIZE, NOT BECAUSE OF
WHAT YOU DO, BUT
BECAUSE OF WHOM
YOU KNOW.

*But now that you have
been freed from sin and
enslaved to God, the advantage
you get is sanctification. The
end is eternal life.*

ROMANS 6:22 NRSV

May 13

THE PRISON HAS BEEN STORMED, AND THE GATES OF THE PRISON HAVE BEEN OPENED, BUT UNLESS WE LEAVE OUR PRISON CELLS AND GO FORWARD INTO THE LIGHT OF FREEDOM, WE ARE STILL UNREDEEMED IN ACTUALITY.

DONALD BLOESCH

For he has rescued us from the dominion of darkness and brought us into the kingdom of the Son he loves.

COLOSSIANS 1:13 NIV

HASN'T CHRIST DONE FOR
YOU WHAT MY PRO-AM
TEAM DID FOR ME? BECAUSE
OF HIS PERFORMANCE, YOU
CLOSE YOUR ROUND WITH A
PERFECT SCORE. DOESN'T
MATTER IF YOU SPRAYED A
FEW INTO THE WOODS OR
SHANKED ONE INTO THE
WATER. WHAT MATTERS IS
THAT YOU SHOWED UP TO
PLAY AND JOINED THE RIGHT
FOURSOME. IN THIS CASE
YOUR FOURSOME IS PRETTY
STRONG; IT'S YOU, THE
FATHER, THE SON, AND THE
HOLY SPIRIT. A BETTER TEAM
DOESN'T EXIST.

August 20

I will ask the Father, and he will

give you another Counselor to be

with you forever—the Spirit

of truth. The world cannot

accept him, because it neither

sees him nor knows him.

But you know him, for he lives

with you and will be in you.

JOHN 14:16-17 NIV

May 14

HAVE WE BEEN GIVEN ANY
GREATER PRIVILEGE THAN
THAT OF CHOICE? NOT
ONLY DOES THIS PRIVILEGE
OFFSET ANY INJUSTICE, THE
GIFT OF FREE WILL CAN
OFFSET ANY MISTAKES.

For he has graciously granted
you the privilege not only
of believing in Christ, but of
suffering for him as well.

PHILIPPIANS 1:29 NRSV

A Pro-Am golf tournament has a simple format. Each team has one pro and four amateurs. The low score from the amateurs is recorded on each hole. Let's take a typical hole where I score an eight but one of the other fellows scores a three. Guess which score is recorded? The three! A person could get used to this! I get credit for the good work of someone else simply by virtue of being on his team.

August 19

In him you also, when you had heard the word of truth, the gospel of your salvation, and had believed in him, were marked with the seal of the promised Holy Spirit; this is the pledge of our inheritance toward redemption as God's own people, to the praise of his glory.

Ephesians 1:13-14 nrsv

THINK ABOUT THE THIEF
WHO REPENTED. HE MADE
SOME BAD MISTAKES IN LIFE.
BUT WOULD YOU CONSIDER
HIS LIFE A WASTE? IS HE
SPENDING ETERNITY
REAPING THE FRUIT OF
ALL THE BAD CHOICES HE
MADE? NO, JUST THE
OPPOSITE. HE IS ENJOYING
THE FRUIT OF THE ONE
GOOD CHOICE HE MADE. IN
THE END ALL HIS BAD
CHOICES WERE REDEEMED
BY A SOLITARY GOOD ONE.

May 15

*Jesus said to him, "I tell you
the truth, today you will
be with me in paradise."*

LUKE 23:43 NIV

August 18

Since we have confidence to enter the sanctuary by the blood of Jesus, by the new and living way that he opened for us through the curtain (that is, through his flesh), and since we have a great priest over the house of God, let us approach with a true heart in full assurance of faith, with our hearts sprinkled clean from an evil conscience and our bodies washed with pure water. Let us hold fast to the confession of our hope without wavering, for he who has promised is faithful.

HEBREWS 10:19–23 NRSV

May 16

Your heavenly Father knows your needs. He will always give

you all you need from day to day if you will make the Kingdom

of God your primary concern. So don't be afraid, little flock.

For it gives your Father great happiness to give you the Kingdom....

Your treasures there will never disappear.... Wherever your

treasure is, there your heart and thoughts will be also.

Luke 12:30-34 tlb

August 17

YET THOUGH THE WORK
OF CHRIST IS FINISHED FOR
THE SINNER, IT IS NOT YET
FINISHED IN THE SINNER.

DONALD G. BLOESCH

*For it is God who works
in you to will and to act
according to his good
purpose...so that you may
become blameless and pure.*

PHILIPPIANS 2:13–14 NIV

You look back over your life and say, "If only...if only I could make up for those bad choices." You can. One good choice for eternity offsets a thousand bad ones on earth. The choice is yours.

Repent therefore and be converted, that your sins may be blotted out, so that times of refreshing may come from the presence of the Lord.

ACTS 3:19 NKJV

August 16

OUR POSITION IS
SUCH THAT WE CAN BE
RESCUED FROM ETERNAL
DEATH AND TRANSLATED
INTO LIFE ONLY BY
TOTAL AND UNCEASING
SUBSTITUTION, THE
SUBSTITUTION WHICH
GOD HIMSELF UNDERTAKES
ON OUR BEHALF.

KARL BARTH

Christ had offered for all time a
single sacrifice for sins....
For by a single offering he has
perfected for all time those
who are sanctified.

HEBREWS 10:12,14 NRSV

How can two brothers be born of the same mother, grow up in the same home, and one choose life and the other choose death? I don't know, but they do. How could two men see the same Jesus and one choose to mock him and the other choose to pray to him? I don't know, but they did. And when one prayed, Jesus loved him enough to save him. And when the other mocked, Jesus loved him enough to let him. He allowed him the choice. He does the same for you.

May 18

He is the atoning sacrifice for our sins, and not only for ours but also for the sins of the whole world.

1 JOHN 2:2 NIV

August 15

God's love was revealed among us in this way: God sent his only

Son into the world so that we might live through him.

This is love: not that we loved God but that he loved us and sent

his Son to be the atoning sacrifice for our sins. Beloved, since

God loved us so much, we also ought to love one another.

1 John 4:9-11 nrsv

May 19

GOD'S PROMISE
IN THE PATH:
I WILL NOT
ABANDON YOU.

Then they led him away

to crucify him.

MATTHEW 27:31 NIV

August 14

GOD'S PROMISE IN THE BLOOD AND WATER: I HAVE REDEEMED YOU AND I WILL KEEP YOU.

To him who is able to keep you from falling and to present you before his glorious presence without fault and with great joy—to the only God our Savior be glory, majesty, power and authority, through Jesus Christ our Lord, before all ages, now and forevermore! Amen.

JUDE 1:24–25 NIV

JESUS ONCE ASKED, IF WE
HUMANS WHO ARE SINFUL
HAVE SUCH A LOVE FOR
OUR CHILDREN, HOW MUCH
MORE DOES GOD, THE
SINLESS AND SELFLESS
FATHER, LOVE US? BUT
WHAT HAPPENS WHEN THE
LOVE ISN'T RETURNED?
WHAT HAPPENS TO THE
HEART OF THE FATHER
WHEN HIS CHILD TURNS
AWAY? ACCORDING TO
THE BIBLE WE HAVE DONE
EXACTLY THAT. WE HAVE
SPURNED THE LOVE OF
OUR FATHER.

May 20

Each of us has gone

his own way.

ISAIAH 53:6 NCV

August 13

But we see Jesus, who was made a little lower than the angels,

now crowned with glory and honor because he suffered death,

so that by the grace of God he might taste death for everyone.

HEBREWS 2:9 NIV

May 21

When we were unable to help ourselves, at the moment of

our need, Christ died for us, although we were living against God.

Very few people will die to save the life of someone else....

But God shows his great love for us in this way:

Christ died for us while we were still sinners.

ROMANS 5:6–8 NCV

A DROWNING SAILOR DOESN'T CALL ON ANOTHER DROWNING SAILOR FOR HELP. A PRISONER DOESN'T BEG ANOTHER PRISONER TO SET HIM FREE. A PAUPER KNOWS BETTER THAN TO BEG FROM ANOTHER PAUPER. HE KNOWS HE NEEDS SOMEONE WHO IS STRONGER THAN HE IS. JESUS' MESSAGE THROUGH THE WINE-SOAKED SPONGE IS THIS: I AM THAT PERSON. TRUST ME.

August 12

For the Son of Man came to seek and to save what was lost.

LUKE 19:10 NIV

Man does, indeed, need a radical change of heart; he needs to begin to hate his sin instead of loving it, and to love God instead of hating him; he needs, in a word, to be reconciled to God. And the place, above all others, where this change takes place is at the foot of the cross, when he apprehends something of the hatred of God for sin and his indescribable love for the sinner.

J. N. D. Anderson

May 22

Not only is this so, but we also rejoice in God through our Lord Jesus Christ, through whom we have now received reconciliation.

Romans 5:11 NIV

His final act is a warm word for the cautious: "You can trust in me." Don't we need someone to trust? And don't we need someone to trust who is bigger than we are? Aren't we tired of trusting the people of this earth for understanding? Aren't we weary of trusting the things of this earth for strength?

August 11

Grace and peace to you from…Jesus Christ, who is the faithful witness, the firstborn from the dead, and the ruler of the kings of the earth.

Revelation 1:4–5 niv

May 23

"WE WERE GOD'S ENEMIES" (ROMANS 5:10). HARSH WORDS, DON'T YOU THINK? AN ENEMY IS AN ADVERSARY. ONE WHO OFFENDS, NOT OUT OF IGNORANCE, BUT BY INTENT. DOES THIS DESCRIBE US? HAVE WE EVER BEEN ENEMIES OF GOD? HAVE WE EVER TURNED AGAINST OUR FATHER?

Don't you know that friendship with the world is hatred toward God? Anyone who chooses to be a friend of the world becomes an enemy of God.

JAMES 4:4 NIV

WHY DID JESUS PROCLAIM HIS THIRST FROM THE CROSS? TO LAY JUST ONE MORE PLANK ON A STURDY BRIDGE OF FULFILLED PROPHECIES OVER WHICH A DOUBTER COULD WALK. HIS CONFESSION OF THIRST IS A SIGNAL FOR ALL WHO SEEK IT—HE IS THE MESSIAH.

August 10

They put gall in my food and gave me vinegar for my thirst.

PSALM 69:21 NIV

May 24

Have you ever done something, knowing God wouldn't want you to do it? Ever hurt one of his children or part of creation? Ever supported or applauded the work of his adversary, the devil? Ever turned against your heavenly Father in public? If so, have you not taken the role of an enemy?

If anyone loves the world,
the love of the Father
is not in him.

1 John 2:15 NIV

Our Lord was concerned with the fulfillment of Scripture. In fact, the fulfillment of Scripture is a recurring theme in the passion. Every important detail of the great tragedy had been written down beforehand. Did you know that in his life Christ fulfilled 332 distinct prophecies in the Old Testament? What are the mathematical possibilities of all these prophecies being fulfilled in the life of one man? 1 in 840,000,000,000,000,000,000,000,000,000,000,000,000,000,000,000,000,000,000,000,000,000,000,000,000,000,000,000,000,000,000,000,000,000,000,000.

August 9

For I tell you, this scripture must be fulfilled in me.

LUKE 22:37 NRSV

SIN IN THE BIBLICAL
PERSPECTIVE IS
POSITIVE REBELLION.

DONALD BLOESCH

May 25

The moment I decide to do good, sin is there to trip me up.

I truly delight in God's commands, but it's pretty obvious that

not all of me joins in that delight. Parts of me covertly

rebel and just when I least expect it they take charge....

Is there no one who can do anything for me?...

The answer, thank God, is that Jesus Christ can and does.

ROMANS 7:21-23,25 MSG

August 8

One of the soldiers pierced his side with a spear, and at once blood and water came out. (He who saw this has testified so that you also may believe. His testimony is true, and he knows that he tells the truth.) These things occurred so that the scripture might be fulfilled, "None of his bones shall be broken." And again another passage of scripture says, "They will look on the one whom they have pierced."

JOHN 19:34–37 NRSV

May 26

If we walk in the light as He Himself is in the Light, we have

fellowship with one another, and the blood of Jesus His Son cleanses

us from all sin.... If we confess our sins, He is faithful and righteous

to forgive us our sins and to cleanse us from all unrighteousness.

1 JOHN 1:7,9 NASB

August 7

Why the recurring references to Scripture? Why, in his final moments was Jesus determined to fulfill prophecy? He knew we would question. And since he did not want our heads to keep his love from our hearts, he used his final moments to offer proof that he was the Messiah. He systematically fulfilled centuries-old prophecies.

When they had carried out all that was written about him, they took him down from the tree and laid him in a tomb.

Acts 13:29 NIV

THE MOST NOTORIOUS
ROAD IN THE WORLD IS THE
VIA DOLOROSA, "THE
WAY OF SORROWS."
ACCORDING TO
TRADITION, IT IS THE
ROUTE JESUS TOOK FROM
PILATE'S HALL TO
CALVARY. NO ONE KNOWS
THE EXACT ROUTE CHRIST
FOLLOWED THAT FRIDAY.
BUT WE DO KNOW WHERE
THE PATH ACTUALLY
BEGAN. THE PATH BEGAN,
NOT IN THE COURT OF
PILATE, BUT IN THE
HALLS OF HEAVEN

May 27

*And all that dwell upon the
earth shall worship him…
the Lamb slain from the
foundation of the world.*

REVELATION 13:8 KJV

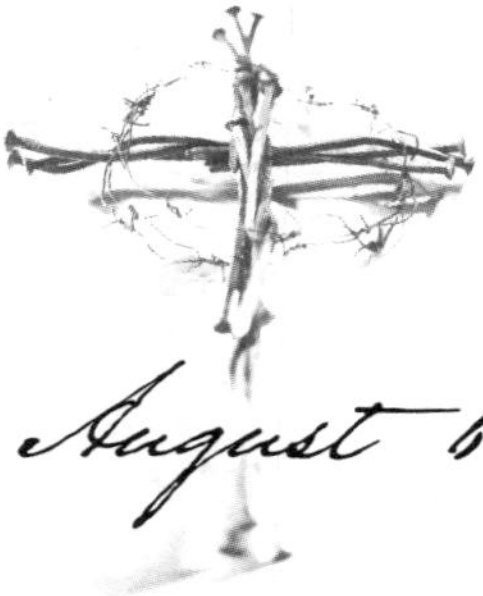

August 6

THE WORD TRUST DOES NOT APPEAR IN THE PASSAGE ABOUT THE WINE AND SPONGE, BUT WE DO FIND A PHRASE THAT MAKES IT EASIER TO TRUST.

So that the Scripture would be fulfilled, Jesus said, "I am thirsty."

JOHN 19:28 NIV

THE FATHER BEGAN HIS
JOURNEY WHEN HE LEFT HIS
HOME IN SEARCH OF US.
ARMED WITH NOTHING
MORE THAN A PASSION TO
WIN YOUR HEART, HE CAME
LOOKING. HIS DESIRE WAS
SINGULAR—TO BRING HIS
CHILDREN HOME. THE BIBLE
HAS A WORD FOR THIS
QUEST: RECONCILIATION.

God was in Christ reconciling
the world to Himself.

2 CORINTHIANS 5:19 NKJV

August 5

Why did the throat of heaven grow raw? So we would know that he understands; so all who struggle would hear his invitation: "You can trust me."

In bringing many sons to glory,
it was fitting that God,
for whom and through whom
everything exists, should make
the author of their salvation
perfect through suffering.

Hebrews 2:10 NIV

THE GREEK WORD
FOR RECONCILE MEANS
"TO RENDER SOMETHING
OTHERWISE."
RECONCILIATION
RESTICHES THE
UNRAVELED, REVERSES
THE REBELLION, REKINDLES
THE COLD PASSION.

May 29

For if, when we were God's enemies, we were reconciled to him through the death of his son, how much more, having been reconciled, shall we be saved through his life!

ROMANS 5:10 NIV

JESUS UNDERSTANDS WHAT
YOU ARE GOING THROUGH.
OUR LORD DOES NOT
PATRONIZE US OR SCOFF AT
OUR NEEDS. HE RESPONDS
"GENEROUSLY TO ALL
WITHOUT FINDING FAULT"
(JAMES 1:5). HOW CAN HE
DO THIS? NO ONE PENNED
IT MORE CLEARLY THAN
DID THE AUTHOR OF
HEBREWS.

August 4

*Jesus understands every
weakness of ours, because he
was tempted in every way that
we are. But he did not sin.*

HEBREWS 4:15 CEV

May 30

RECONCILIATION TOUCHES
THE SHOULDER OF THE
WAYWARD AND WOOS
HIM HOMEWARD.

Come to me, all you who are
weary and burdened, and I
will give you rest.

MATTHEW 11:28 NIV

August 3

I will have mercy on whom I have mercy, and I will have compassion on whom I have compassion. It does not, therefore, depend on man's desire or effort, but on God's mercy.

<small>ROMANS 9:15-16 NIV</small>

May 31

All sin can do is threaten us with death, and that's the

end of it. Grace, because God is putting everything

together again through the Messiah, invites us into life—

a life that goes on and on and on, world without end.

ROMANS 5:21 MSG

August 2

JESUS HAS BEEN WHERE YOU
ARE AND CAN RELATE TO
HOW YOU FEEL. AND IF HIS
LIFE ON EARTH DOESN'T
CONVINCE YOU, HIS DEATH
ON THE CROSS SHOULD.

For the Lord comforts his
people and will have
compassion on his afflicted ones.

ISAIAH 49:13 NIV

June 1

THE PATH TO THE CROSS
TELLS US EXACTLY HOW
FAR GOD WILL GO TO CALL
US BACK.

He humbled himself and
became obedient to death—
even death on a cross!

PHILIPPIANS 2:8 NIV

DOESN'T THE LACK OF
UNDERSTANDING KEEP US FROM
OTHERS? SUPPOSE YOU WERE
DISCOURAGED AT YOUR
FINANCIAL STATE. YOU NEED
SOME GUIDANCE FROM A
SYMPATHETIC FRIEND. WOULD
YOU GO TO THE SON OF A
ZILLIONAIRE? (REMEMBER,
YOU'RE ASKING FOR GUIDANCE,
NOT A HANDOUT.) WOULD YOU
APPROACH SOMEONE WHO
INHERITED A FORTUNE?
PROBABLY NOT. WHY? HE
WOULD NOT UNDERSTAND.
HE'S LIKELY NEVER BEEN WHERE
YOU ARE, SO HE CAN'T RELATE
TO HOW YOU FEEL.

August 1

If any of you lacks wisdom,
he should ask God, who gives
generously to all without
finding fault, and it
will be given to him.
JAMES 1:5 NIV

THEY APPEAR SO
DIFFERENT. PRIDE PUFFS
OUT HER CHEST. SHAME
HANGS HER HEAD. YOU'D
NEVER KNOW THEY
ARE SISTERS. BUT DON'T
BE FOOLED, THE EMOTIONS
HAVE THE SAME PARENTAGE.
AND THE SAME IMPACT.
THEY KEEP YOU FROM
YOUR FATHER. PRIDE DRIVES
YOU AWAY. SHAME KEEPS
YOU AWAY. IF PRIDE IS
WHAT GOES BEFORE A FALL,
THEN SHAME IS WHAT
KEEPS YOU FROM GETTING
UP AFTER ONE.

June 2

Pride goes before destruction,
and a haughty spirit
before a fall.
PROVERBS 16:18 NRSV

July 31

BECAUSE HE UNDERSTANDS,
WE CAN COME TO HIM.

So whenever we are in need,
we should come bravely
before the throne of our
merciful God. There we will
be treated with undeserved
kindness, and we will find help.

HEBREWS 4:16 CEV

June 3

GOD'S PROMISE
IN THE GARMENT:
I WILL GIVE
YOU MY ROBE.

They divided his clothes among the four of them. They also took his robe, but it was seamless, woven in one piece from the top. So they said, "Let's not tear it but throw dice to see who gets it."

JOHN 19:23–24 NLT

JESUS KNEW YOU WOULD BE
WEARY, DISTURBED, AND
ANGRY. HE KNEW YOU'D BE
SLEEPY, GRIEF-STRICKEN,
AND HUNGRY. HE KNEW
YOU'D FACE PAIN. IF NOT
THE PAIN OF THE BODY, THE
PAIN OF THE SOUL...PAIN
TOO SHARP FOR ANY
DRUG. HE KNEW YOU'D
FACE THIRST. IF NOT A
THIRST FOR WATER, AT
LEAST A THIRST FOR
TRUTH, AND THE TRUTH WE
GLEAN FROM THE IMAGE OF
A THIRSTY CHRIST—HE
UNDERSTANDS.

July 30

*Blessed are you when
people revile you and
persecute you and utter
all kinds of evil against you
falsely on my account.*

MATTHEW 5:11 NRSV

THE MAÎTRE D' WOULDN'T CHANGE HIS MIND. I WASN'T WEARING A JACKET. DIDN'T KNOW I NEEDED ONE. "THERE'S GOT TO BE SOMETHING YOU CAN DO," I PLEADED. HE DISAPPEARED INTO THE CLOAKROOM AND EMERGED WITH A JACKET. I NEEDED A JACKET, BUT ALL I HAD WAS A PRAYER. THE FELLOW WAS TOO KIND TO TURN ME AWAY BUT TOO LOYAL TO LOWER THE STANDARD. SO THE VERY ONE WHO REQUIRED A JACKET GAVE ME A JACKET, AND WE WERE GIVEN A TABLE. ISN'T THIS WHAT HAPPENED AT THE CROSS?

June 4

From his fullness we have all received, grace upon grace.

JOHN 1:16 NRSV

July 29

So Jesus said to them, "Very truly, I tell you, unless you eat
the flesh of the Son of Man and drink his blood, you have no
life in you. Those who eat my flesh and drink my blood have
eternal life, and I will raise them up on the last day; for my
flesh is true food and my blood is true drink. Those who
eat my flesh and drink my blood abide in me, and I in them."

JOHN 6:53–56 NRSV

June 5

For we ourselves were once foolish, disobedient, led astray, slaves to various passions and pleasures…. But when the goodness and loving kindness of God our Savior appeared, he saved us, not because of any works of righteousness that we had done, but according to his mercy, through the water of rebirth and renewal by the Holy Spirit.

TITUS 3:3-5 NRSV

WHY DID HE ENDURE ALL THESE FEELINGS? BECAUSE HE KNEW YOU WOULD FEEL THEM TOO. WHY DID JESUS GROW WEARY IN SAMARIA (JOHN 4:6), DISTURBED IN NAZARETH (MARK 6:6), AND ANGRY IN THE TEMPLE (JOHN 2:15)? WHY WAS HE SLEEPY IN THE BOAT ON GALILEE (MARK 4:38), SAD AT THE TOMB OF LAZARUS (JOHN 11:35), AND HUNGRY IN THE WILDERNESS (MATTHEW 4:2)?

July 28

Because he himself suffered when he was tempted, he is able to help those who are being tempted.

HEBREWS 2:18 NIV

Seats at God's table are not available to the sloppy. But who among us is anything but? Unkempt morality. Untidy with truth. Careless with people. Our moral clothing is in disarray. Yes, the standard for sitting at God's table is high, but the love of God for his children is higher. So he offers a gift. Not a garment pulled out of a cloakroom but a robe worn by his son, Jesus.

June 6

But if Christ is in you, though the body is dead because of sin, the Spirit is life because of righteousness.

Romans 8:10 NRSV

July 27

Six hours before the wine-soaked sponge, Jesus had been offered drink, but he refused it. Mark says the wine was mixed with myrrh. Matthew described it as wine mixed with gall. Both myrrh and gall contain sedative properties that numb the senses. But Jesus refused them. He refused to be stupefied by the drugs, opting instead to feel the full force of his suffering.

There they offered Jesus wine to drink, mixed with gall; but after tasting it, he refused to drink it.

MATTHEW 27:34 NIV

June 7

THIS IS THE MYSTERY OF
THE RICHES OF DIVINE
GRACE FOR SINNERS;
FOR BY A WONDERFUL
EXCHANGE OUR SINS ARE
NOW NOT OURS BUT
CHRIST'S, AND CHRIST'S
RIGHTEOUSNESS IS NOT
CHRIST'S BUT OURS.

MARTIN LUTHER

*You know the grace of our
Lord Jesus Christ. You know
that Christ was rich, but for
you he became poor so
that by his becoming poor
you might become rich.*

2 CORINTHIANS 8:9 NCV

July 26

He is thirsty. Why doesn't he do something about it? Couldn't he? Did he not cause jugs of water to be jugs of wine? Did God not say, "I will pour water on him who is thirsty" (Isa. 44:3)? If so, why does Jesus endure thirst? Because he knew you'd face thirst too.

When Jesus knew that all was now finished, he said (in order to fulfill the scripture), "I am thirsty."

John 19:28 NRSV

June 8

A SEAMLESS ROBE. IT MUST HAVE BEEN JESUS' FINEST POSSESSION. WHY IS THIS SIGNIFICANT? SCRIPTURE OFTEN DESCRIBES OUR BEHAVIOR AS THE CLOTHES WE WEAR. GARMENTS CAN SYMBOLIZE CHARACTER, AND LIKE HIS GARMENT, JESUS' CHARACTER WAS SEAMLESS. COORDINATED. UNIFIED. HE WAS LIKE HIS ROBE: UNINTERRUPTED PERFECTION.

This garment was seamless, woven in one piece from top to bottom.

JOHN 19:23 NIV

JESUS. LIPS CRACKED AND MOUTH OF COTTON. THROAT SO DRY HE COULDN'T SWALLOW, AND VOICE SO HEARSE HE COULD SCARCELY SPEAK. HE IS THIRSTY. TO FIND THE LAST TIME MOISTURE TOUCHED THESE LIPS YOU NEED TO REWIND A DOZEN HOURS TO THE MEAL IN THE UPPER ROOM. SINCE TASTING THAT CUP OF WINE, JESUS HAS BEEN BEATEN, SPAT UPON, BRUISED, AND CUT. HE HAS BEEN A CROSS-CARRIER AND SIN-BEARER, AND NO LIQUID HAS SALVED HIS THROAT. HE IS THIRSTY.

July 25

They plaited a crown from branches of a thorn bush and set it on his head. They put a stick in his right hand for a scepter.... Then they spit on him and hit him on the head with the stick.

MATTHEW 27:29–30 MSG

June 9

Jesus' robe was
"woven...from the top."
Jesus wasn't led by his
own mind; he was led by
the mind of his Father.

The Son can do nothing
on his own, but only what
he sees the Father doing;
for whatever the Father does,
the Son does likewise.

John 5:19 nrsv

July 24

Praise be to the God and Father of our Lord Jesus Christ,

the Father of compassion and the God of all comfort, who

comforts us in all our troubles, so that we can comfort those

in any trouble with the comfort we ourselves have received

from God. For just as the sufferings of Christ flow over into

our lives, so also through Christ our comfort overflows.

2 Corinthians 1:3–5 niv

June 10

Much more surely then, now that we have been justified

by his blood, will we be saved through him from the wrath of God.

For if while we were enemies, we were reconciled to

God through the death of his Son, much more surely,

having been reconciled, will we be saved by his life.

ROMANS 5:9–10 NRSV

EVEN JESUS' FINAL ACT ON EARTH WAS INTENDED TO WIN YOUR TRUST. IN THE CONCLUDING MEASURE OF HIS EARTHLY COMPOSITION, WE HEAR THE SOUNDS OF A THIRSTY MAN. AND THROUGH HIS THIRST HE LEAVES A FINAL APPEAL. "YOU CAN TRUST ME."

July 23

God didn't go to all the trouble of sending his Son merely to point an accusing finger, telling the world how bad it was. He came to help, to put the world right again. Anyone who trusts in him is acquitted; anyone who refuses to trust him has long since been under the death sentence without knowing it. And why? Because of that person's failure to believe in the one-of-a-kind Son of God when introduced to him.

JOHN 3:17-18 MSG

THE CHARACTER OF JESUS WAS A SEAMLESS FABRIC WOVEN FROM HEAVEN TO EARTH...FROM GOD'S THOUGHTS TO JESUS' ACTIONS. FROM GOD'S TEARS TO JESUS' COMPASSION. FROM GOD'S WORD TO JESUS' RESPONSE. ALL ONE PIECE. ALL A PICTURE OF THE CHARACTER OF JESUS.

June 11

What my Father has given me is greater than all else, and no one can snatch it out of the Father's hand. The Father and I are one.

JOHN 10:29–30 NRSV

WHY DID JESUS LIVE ON THE
EARTH AS LONG AS HE DID?
COULDN'T HIS LIFE HAVE
BEEN MUCH SHORTER?
WHY NOT STEP INTO OUR
WORLD JUST LONG ENOUGH
TO DIE FOR OUR SINS AND
THEN LEAVE? TO TAKE ON
OUR SINS IS ONE THING,
BUT TO TAKE ON OUR
SUNBURNS, OUR SORE
THROATS? TO EXPERIENCE
DEATH, YES—BUT TO PUT
UP WITH LIFE? WHY DID HE
DO IT? BECAUSE HE WANTS
YOU TO TRUST HIM.

July 22

*Commit your way to the Lord;
trust in him, and he will act.*

PSALM 37:5 NRSV

June 12

When Christ was nailed to the cross, he took off his robe of seamless perfection and assumed a different wardrobe, the wardrobe of indignity. The indignity of nakedness. The indignity of failure. Worst of all, the indignity of sin.

He himself bore our sins in his body on the tree, so that we might die to sins and live for righteousness.

1 Peter 2:24 NIV

July 21

GOD'S PROMISE IN THE
WINE-SOAKED SPONGE:
I UNDERSTAND
YOUR PAIN.

*For we do not have a high priest
who is unable to sympathize
with our weaknesses, but we
have one who has been tempted
in every way, just as we are—
yet was without sin.*

HEBREWS 4:15 NIV

June 13

THE CLOTHING OF CHRIST
ON THE CROSS? SIN—
YOURS AND MINE. THE SINS
OF ALL HUMANITY.

We all, like sheep, have gone

astray, each of us had turned

to his own way; and the

Lord has laid on him

the iniquity of us all.

ISAIAH 53:6 NIV

July 20

Don't trust your conscience. Trust the cross. The blood has been spilt and the veil has been split. You are welcome in God's presence.

Who is he that condemns? Christ Jesus, who died— more than that, who was raised to life—is at the right hand of God and is also interceding for us.

Romans 8:34 NIV

I CAN REMEMBER MY FATHER
EXPLAINING TO ME THE
REASON A GROUP OF MEN
ON THE SIDE OF THE ROAD
WORE STRIPED CLOTHING.
"THEY'RE PRISONERS," HE
SAID. "THEY HAVE BROKEN
THE LAW." YOU WANT TO
KNOW WHAT STUCK WITH ME
ABOUT THESE MEN? THEY
NEVER LOOKED UP. THEY
NEVER MADE EYE CONTACT.
WERE THEY ASHAMED?
PROBABLY SO. WHAT THEY
FELT ON THE SIDE OF THE
ROAD WAS WHAT OUR
SAVIOR FELT ON THE
CROSS—DISGRACE.

June 14

*See, I have taken away
your sin, and I will put
rich garments on you.*

ZECHARIAH 3:4 NIV

July 19

God our Savior, who desires everyone to be saved and to come to the knowledge of the truth. For there is one God; there is also one mediator between God and humankind, Christ Jesus, himself human, who gave himself a ransom for all—this was attested at the right time.

1 Timothy 2:3–6 NRSV

June 15

God presented [Jesus] as a sacrifice of atonement, through faith in his blood. He did this to demonstrate his justice, because in his forbearance he had left the sins committed beforehand unpunished—he did it to demonstrate his justice at the present time, so as to be just and the one who justifies those who have faith in Jesus.

ROMANS 3:24–26 NIV

July 18

GOD WELCOMES YOU. GOD
IS NOT AVOIDING YOU.
GOD IS NOT RESISTING
YOU. THE CURTAIN IS
DOWN, THE DOOR IS OPEN,
AND GOD INVITES YOU IN.

"Come now, let us reason
together," says the Lord.
"Though your sins are like
scarlet, they shall be as white
as snow; though they are red as
crimson, they shall be like wool."

ISAIAH 1:18 NIV

June 16

BUT CHRIST WITHOUT
GUILT...TOOK UPON HIMSELF
OUR PUNISHMENT, IN
ORDER THAT HE MIGHT
THUS EXPIATE OUR GUILT,
AND DO AWAY WITH OUR
PUNISHMENT.

AUGUSTINE

For Christ died for sins
once for all, the righteous
for the unrighteous,
to bring you to God.

1 PETER 3:18 NIV

GOD ISN'T ANGRY WITH
YOU. HE HAS ALREADY
DEALT WITH YOUR
MISTAKES. SOMEWHERE,
SOMETIME, SOMEHOW
YOU GOT TANGLED UP IN
GARBAGE, AND YOU'VE
BEEN AVOIDING GOD.
YOU'VE ALLOWED A VEIL
OF GUILT TO COME
BETWEEN YOU AND YOUR
FATHER. YOU WONDER IF
YOU COULD EVER FEEL
CLOSE TO GOD AGAIN.
THE MESSAGE OF THE
TORN FLESH IS YOU CAN.

July 17

My presence will go with you,
and I will give you rest.

EXODUS 33:14 NIV

EVERY ASPECT OF
THE CRUCIFIXION WAS
INTENDED NOT ONLY TO
HURT THE VICTIM BUT TO
SHAME HIM. DEATH ON A
CROSS WAS USUALLY
RESERVED FOR
THE MOST VILE OFFENDERS:
SLAVES, MURDERERS,
ASSASSINS, AND THE LIKE.
JESUS WAS NOT ONLY
SHAMED BEFORE PEOPLE,
HE WAS SHAMED BEFORE
HEAVEN.

June 17

He suffered death on the cross.
But he accepted the shame as if
it were nothing because of the
joy that God put before him.
And now he is sitting at the
right side of God's throne.

HEBREWS 12:2 NCV

July 16

We have a tendency to put the barrier that separates us from God back up. Though there is no curtain in a temple, there is a curtain in the heart. Like the ticks on the clock are the mistakes of the heart. And sometimes, no, oftentimes, we allow those mistakes to keep us from God. Our guilty conscience becomes a curtain that separates us from God. As a result we hide from our Master.

Dear children, continue in him, so that when he appears we may be confident and unashamed before him at his coming.

1 JOHN 2:28 NIV

June 18

Since he bore the sin of the murderer and adulterer, he felt the shame of the murderer and adulterer. Though he never lied, he bore the disgrace of a liar. Though he never cheated, he felt the embarrassment of a cheater. Since he bore the sin of the world, he felt the collective shame of the world.

So let us go out to him outside the camp and bear the disgrace he bore.

Hebrews 13:13 nlt

July 15

And for us? What did the torn curtain signify for us? We are welcome to enter into God's presence—any day, any time. God has removed the barrier that separates us from him. The barrier of sin? Down. He has removed the curtain.

Since we have a great priest over the house of God, let us draw near to God with a sincere heart in full assurance of faith.

HEBREWS 10:21–22 NIV

June 19

WHILE ON THE CROSS,
JESUS FELT THE INDIGNITY
AND DISGRACE OF A
CRIMINAL. NO, HE WAS
NOT GUILTY. NO, HE HAD
NOT COMMITTED A SIN.
AND, NO, HE DID NOT
DESERVE TO BE SENTENCED.
BUT YOU AND I WERE, WE
HAD, AND WE DID.

*But you know that he appeared
so that he might take away our
sins. And in him is no sin.*

1 JOHN 3:5 NIV

July 14

Death reigned from the time of Adam to the time of Moses, even over those who did not sin by breaking a command, as did Adam, who was a pattern of the one to come. But the gift is not like the trespass. For if the many died by the trespass of the one man, how much more did God's grace and the gift that came by the grace of the one man, Jesus Christ, overflow to the many! Again, the gift of God is not like the result of the one man's sin: The judgement followed one sin and brought condemnation, but the gift followed many trespasses and brought justification.

ROMANS 5:14–16 NIV

June 20

Think about Jesus' example. He held on while wicked

people were doing evil things to him. So do not get tired

and stop trying. You are struggling against sin, but your struggles

have not yet caused you to be killed.... So hold on through

your sufferings, because they are like a father's discipline.

HEBREWS 12:3–4, 7 NCV

July 13

What did the torn curtain mean? For the Jews it meant no more barrier between them and the Holy of Holies. No more priests to go between them and God. No more animal sacrifices to atone for their sins.

We have this hope as an anchor for the soul, firm and secure. It enters the inner sanctuary behind the curtain, where Jesus, who went before us, has entered on our behalf. He has become a high priest forever.

Hebrews 6:19–20 niv

June 21

JESUS OFFERS A ROBE OF
SEAMLESS PURITY AND
DONS MY PATCHWORK
COAT OF PRIDE, GREED,
AND SELFISHNESS. HE WORE
OUR SIN SO WE COULD
WEAR HIS RIGHTEOUSNESS.

He changed places with us.

GALATIANS 3:13 NCV

July 12

Keep in mind the size of the curtain—sixty feet tall and thirty feet wide. One instant it was whole; the next it was ripped in two from top to bottom. No delay. No hesitation.

The Lord is not slow in keeping his promise...not wanting anyone to perish, but everyone to come to repentance.

2 Peter 3:9 niv

June 22

THOUGH WE COME TO THE CROSS DRESSED IN SIN, WE LEAVE THE CROSS DRESSED IN THE "COAT OF HIS STRONG LOVE."

He covered himself with goodness like armor. He put the helmet of salvation on his head. He put on the clothes of punishment and wrapped himself in the coat of his strong love.

ISAIAH 59:17 NCV

July 11

What appeared to be the cruelty of man was actually the sovereignty of God. It's as if the hands of heaven had been gripping the veil of the temple, waiting for this moment when it would be ripped in two from top to bottom.

And when Jesus had cried out again in a loud voice, he gave up his spirit. At that moment the curtain of the temple was torn in two from top to bottom.

MATTHEW 27:50–51 NIV

June 23

THOUGH WE COME TO THE CROSS DRESSED IN SIN, WE LEAVE THE CROSS GIRDED WITH A BELT OF "GOODNESS AND FAIRNESS."

Goodness and fairness will give him strength, like a belt around his waist.

ISAIAH 11:5 NCV

July 10

JESUS HASN'T LEFT US WITH
AN UNAPPROACHABLE
GOD. YES, GOD IS HOLY.
YES, WE ARE SINFUL. BUT,
YES, YES, YES, JESUS IS
OUR MEDIATOR. IS NOT A
MEDIATOR ONE WHO "GOES
BETWEEN"? WASN'T JESUS
THE CURTAIN BETWEEN US
AND GOD? AND WASN'T
HIS FLESH TORN?

*There is one God and one
mediator between God and
men, the man Christ Jesus.*

1 TIMOTHY 2:5 NIV

June 24

*Through [Jesus] God was pleased to reconcile to himself
all things, whether on earth or in heaven, by making peace
through the blood of his cross. And you who were once
estranged and hostile in mind, doing evil deeds, he has
now reconciled in his fleshly body through death, so as to
present you holy and blameless and irreproachable before him.*

COLOSSIANS 1:20–22 NRSV

July 9

For the grace of God that brings salvation has appeared to all men.
It teaches us to say "No" to ungodliness and worldly passions,
and to live self-controlled, upright and godly lives in this present age,
while we wait for the blessed hope—the glorious appearing of our
great God and Savior, Jesus Christ, who gave himself for us to
redeem us from all wickedness and to purify for himself a
people that are his very own, eager to do what is good.

TITUS 2:11–14 NIV

June 25

THOUGH WE COME TO THE CROSS DRESSED IN SIN, WE LEAVE THE CROSS CLOTHED IN "GARMENTS OF SALVATION."

I delight greatly in the Lord; my soul rejoices in my God. For he has clothed me with garments of salvation and arrayed me in a robe of righteousness, as a bridegroom adorns his head like a priest, and as a bride adorns herself with her jewels.

ISAIAH 61:10 NIV

July 8

We know God is good.
We know we are not,
and we feel far from
God. The ancient
words of Job are ours,
"If only there were a
mediator who could
bring us together"
(Job 9:33). Oh,
but there is!

For he hath made him to be
sin for us, who knew no sin;
that we might be made the
righteousness of God in him.

2 Corinthians 5:21 kjv

June 26

And you, child, will be called the prophet of the Most High;

for you will go before the Lord to prepare his ways, to give

knowledge of salvation to his people by the forgiveness of

their sins. By the tender mercy of our God, the dawn from on high

will break upon us, to give light to those who sit in darkness and in

the shadow of death, to guide our feet into the way of peace.

<small>LUKE 1:76–79 NRSV</small>

July 7

God, the blessed and only Ruler, the King of kings and Lord of lords, who alone is immortal and who lives in unapproachable light, whom no one has seen or can see. To him be honor and might forever.

1 Timothy 6:15–16 NIV

June 27

Though we come to the cross dressed in sin, we leave the cross indeed, we leave dressed in Christ himself.

Baptized into union with him, you have all put on Christ as a garment.

Galatians 3:27 NEB

NO ONE BUT THE HIGH
PRIEST ENTERED THE HOLY
OF HOLIES. NO ONE. TO DO
SO MEANT DEATH. IN NO
UNCERTAIN TERMS, THE
CURTAIN DECLARED: "THIS
FAR AND NO FARTHER!"
FIFTEEN HUNDRED YEARS
OF A CURTAIN-DRAPED
HOLY OF HOLIES
COMMUNICATED THAT
GOD IS HOLY...SEPARATE
FROM US AND
UNAPPROACHABLE.

July 6

The Lord said to Moses:
Tell your brother Aaron not to
come just at any time into the
sanctuary inside the curtain
before the mercy seat that is
upon the ark, or he will die;
for I appear in the cloud
upon the mercy seat.

LEVITICUS 16:2 NRSV

June 28

It wasn't enough for Jesus to prepare you a feast. It wasn't enough for him to reserve you a seat. It wasn't enough for him to cover the cost and provide the transportation to the banquet. He did something more. He let you wear his own clothes so that you would be properly dressed. He did that... just for you.

Blessed are those who hunger and thirst for righteousness, for they will be filled.

MATTHEW 5:6 NIV

THE CURTAIN OF THE
TEMPLE IS THE VEIL THAT
HUNG BEFORE THE HOLY
OF HOLIES. THE HOLY OF
HOLIES, YOU'LL REMEMBER,
WAS A PART OF THE
TEMPLE NO ONE COULD
ENTER BECAUSE THE
SHEKINAH GLORY—THE
GLORY OF GOD—WAS
PRESENT THERE. NOW
NOTHING REMAINS
BETWEEN YOU AND GOD
BUT AN OPEN DOOR.

July 5

*A large outer tent was set up.
The lampstand, the table, and
"the bread of presence" were
placed in it. This was called "the
Holy Place." Then a curtain was
stretched, and behind it a smaller,
inside tent set up. This was called
"the Holy of Holies."*

HEBREWS 9:2-3 MSG

June 29

Blessed be the God and Father of our Lord Jesus Christ!

By his great mercy he has given us a new birth into a living hope

through the resurrection of Jesus Christ from the dead, and into an

inheritance that is imperishable, undefiled, and unfading,

kept in heaven for you, who are being protected by the power of God

through faith for a salvation ready to be revealed in the last time.

1 PETER 1:3–5 NRSV

July 4

While they [disciples] were eating, Jesus took a loaf of bread,
and after blessing it he broke it, gave it to the disciples, and said,
"Take, eat; this is my body." Then he took a cup, and after giving
thanks he gave it to them, saying, "Drink from it, all of you;
for this is my blood of the covenant, which is poured
out for many for the forgiveness of sins.

MATTHEW 26:26-28 NRSV

June 30

GOD'S PROMISE
THROUGH THE TORN FLESH:
I INVITE YOU
INTO MY PRESENCE.

*We can enter through a new
and living way that Jesus
opened for us. It leads through
the curtain—Christ's body.*

HEBREWS 10:20 NCV

ACCORDING TO THE
WRITER, THE CURTAIN
EQUALS JESUS. HENCE,
WHATEVER HAPPENED
TO THE FLESH OF JESUS
HAPPENED TO THE CURTAIN.
HIS FLESH WAS TORN BY
THE WHIPS, TORN BY THE
THORNS. TORN BY THE
WEIGHT OF THE CROSS AND
THE POINT OF THE NAILS.
BUT IN THE HORROR
OF HIS TORN FLESH, WE
FIND THE SPLENDOR OF
THE OPEN DOOR.

July 3

*For through him we
both have access to the
Father by one Spirit.*

EPHESIANS 2:18 NIV

July 1

GOD HAS HEARD YOU, AND
HE HAS INVITED YOU.
WHAT ONCE SEPARATED
YOU HAS BEEN REMOVED.
NOTHING REMAINS
BETWEEN YOU AND GOD
BUT AN OPEN DOOR.

Now in Christ Jesus,
you who were far away from
God are brought near.

EPHESIANS 2:13 NCV

July 2

SOMEONE OPENED THE CURTAIN. SOMEONE TORE DOWN THE VEIL. SOMETHING HAPPENED IN THE DEATH OF CHRIST THAT OPENED THE DOOR FOR YOU AND ME.

Let us then approach the throne of grace with confidence, so that we may receive mercy and find grace to help us in our time of need.

HEBREWS 4:16 NIV